THE
FINANCIAL SECTOR
OF THE AMERICAN
ECONOMY

edited by

STUART BRUCHEY
UNIVERSITY OF MAINE

A GARLAND SERIES

STOCK EXCHANGE AUTOMATION

JAMAL MUNSHI

GARLAND PUBLISHING, INC.
NEW YORK & LONDON / 1994

Library of Congress Cataloging-in-Publication Data

Munshi, Jamal.
    Stock exchange automation / Jamal Munshi.
        p.   cm. — (The Financial sector of the American economy)
    Includes bibliographical references and index.
    ISBN 0–8153–1702–6
    1. Program trading (Securities)—Data processing. 2. Stock-
exchange—Communication systems.   I. Title. II. Series.
HG4515.5.M86 1994
332.64'0285—dc20   94–483
                                      CIP

Printed on acid-free, 250-year-life paper
Manufactured in the United States of America

Contents

An Overview of Capital Markets and of the Nature of this Investigation

Does computerization of trading affect price behavior? Market microstructure theory implies that at least some forms of automation should affect prices. Theories of price formation in the specialist based trading system postulate that the trading mechanism induces short term price volatility. In this paper we examine these effects and in the empirical portion of this work we investigate the implementation of the electronic trading system that has recently been installed on the floor of the NYSE; (New York Stock Exchange). The testable implication is that the intraday volatility of stocks traded on the 'electronic book' will differ from those traded on the manual book.

The motivation for this study derives from the pivotal role played by capital markets in market economies. Capital markets are an essential component of the free market system. They function as allocators of investable funds among competing uses. The movement toward automated markets requires that we understand how automation changes market behavior. This study provides empirical evidence to market designers, researchers, and regulators to assist them in accurately assessing these changes.

HOW THE IMPACT OF I.T. IS MEASURED

Information systems are costly to purchase, deploy, and maintain. Therefore, in a world where business enterprise is operated for value maximization according to the theory of rational choice it is natural to suppose that information technology offers economic value and that this value overcomes the costs. However, convincing empirical evidence in support of the economic value of information systems has not been available to date (see for example, Crowston and Treacy 1986) and the need for such evidence occupies the highest priority in the IT research agenda (Miller 1989).

The reasons for such an agenda have to do with economic efficiency and global competitiveness. For an economy to be efficient, it must optimize use of all resources including information technology or IT. Inappropriate investment in IT, whether it be insufficient or excessive, represents misallocation of funds. The role played by IT in economic growth is seen by many scholars to be gaining in importance since the U.S. is considered to be in the process of shifting from an industrial economy to an information economy. Jonscher (1983) provides the most quoted and the definitive analysis of this scenario.

Empirical research in IT effectiveness has been extensive and dates back at least to the early '70s (Lucas 1975a, 1975b). Such research seeks to determine whether the implementation of information systems has a tangible and measurable impact on the business enterprise. A comprehensive literature review and meta analysis of this body of work can be found in Crowston and Treacy (1986), Miller (1989) and Melone (1989). These studies show that the bulk of research in IT effectiveness has been subjective rather than objective. They rely only on questionnaires that elicit opinions and attitudes rather than on direct observation.

The most popular subjective measure is that of "user information satisfaction" or UIS. This measure was first suggested by Noland and Seward (1974) in their book on managing information systems and was apparently meant to provide a tool to IT managers to evaluate information systems in-house. The method was extended for use in cross sectional studies by Bailey and Pearson (1983) who defined a set of 39 factors for system evaluation. This paper kicked off an avalanche of UIS research that continues unabated though not without controversy. Melone (1989), for example, finds UIS research to be methodologically flawed and the so called "UIS construct" to be inadequate as a measure of system effectiveness.

Opinion survey research instruments have also been used as a substitute for direct observation of variables such as system usage, implementation success, and system value. For example, Srinavasan (1986) has used opinion surveys to determine usage and to assess the correlation between usage and UIS while Gallagher (1974) has used a similar technique to assess the 'value' of an information system. Sethi and King (1991) have recently proposed a 'construct' that may be used in opinion research of this form for assessing the effectiveness of information systems.

Another class of researchers of IT effectiveness has eschewed the subjective opinion survey approach and has called for empirical research of directly observable measures of IT effectiveness such as efficiency and profitability of business enterprise. Rather than satisfaction, usage, or managerial opinions of the value of the information system, "effectiveness" is seen by these researchers as the extent to which managers can "convert IT investment into useful output" (Weill and Olson 1989); the "impact of IT on the bottom line of business" (Crowston and Treacy 1986); and the "relationship between the use of a system and performance" of the users in terms of rational objectives of the business (Lucas 1975).

Conventional cross sectional studies of this nature have been inconclusive (Cron and Sobol 1983, Stabell 1983, Strassman 1984, Chismar and Kriebel 1985, Floyd and Wooldridge 1990) possibly because of the difficulty of defining the dependent variables and measuring the level of IT investment in a manner that would apply uniformly to a large cross section of firms and systems. Bakos (1987) contains a discussion of the dependent variable problem. An added problem is the effect of intervening variables that cannot easily be controlled in a large cross sectional field study although some studies such as Floyd and Wooldridge (1990) have made some progress in this direction.

A possible remedy is to move the study to a controlled laboratory where a treatment group is allowed to use a certain information system to solve a hypothetical business problem while a control group solves the same problem without the system. Objective measures of solution quality are defined and obtained by direct observation. King and Rodriguez (1978) is exemplary of such studies. But there is a tradeoff involved. The gain in internal validity and reliability is offset by a lack of realism in the experimental setting and the relative inability to externalize and generalize the findings to a large class of users or systems in the field.

The external validity of a controlled study is considerably higher in a "scientific case study" described by Lee (1989) and Benbasat, Goldstein, and Mead (1987). The experiment is moved out of the laboratory back to the field but the emphasis is on surgical precision rather than sample size. The archetype of the case study in effectiveness is that of Markus (1983) although Lucas (1975) also fits the model and predates the Markus study considerably. The validity of such a study is based on the argument that if the model is correctly specified and the variables involved can be controlled experimentally by 'fortuitous circumstances' as in Markus (1983), observations made without measurement error in a single case study can be used to reject a hypothesis. Lee (1989) offers examples from the natural sciences to support the use of this methodology in IT research.

A modified form of such a study is undertaken here to assess the impact of computerized trading in securities markets. A conventional cross sectional study would require the analysis of gross measures of the success, competitiveness, or efficiency of a large sample of exchanges in relation to the level of investment in information technology and allow the size and randomness of the sample to even out the effects of uncontrolled variables. In contrast, the case study methodology would focus on a controlled study of a single implementation in one market. The present study is able to combine the properties of both methods because of a fortuitous implementation schedule.

The study seeks to assess the impact on price volatility and asset liquidity of the phased implementation of the Electronic Book on the floor of the New York Stock Exchange. Over a period of three years from 1987 through 1989, several hundred stocks were converted to electronic trading a few at a time. Each stock can be considered to be a market (eg, the market for IBM stock rather than the stock market as a whole). Thus, within a controlled microstructure (the NYSE specialist system) and type of automation (the Electronic Book) it is possible to establish conventional statistical tests over a sample of implementations.

THE THEORY OF CAPITAL MARKETS

In a market economy allocation of capital to competing projects is made according to the laws of supply and demand which determine the investors' required rate of return from each project. The allocative efficiency of the system is improved by the existence of capital markets which provide liquidity to holders of capital assets. Their success, performance, and efficiency are therefore measured by the extent to which they provide depth and speed of execution as well as by their ability to disseminate trade information rapidly to all participants at a minimum cost. The cost includes search costs, information costs, execution costs, and market impact costs. Hasbrouck and Schwartz (1988) discusses the inefficiencies induced into market mechanisms by execution costs.

To perform its function, the market must communicate market price information to the traders, route their orders to the market, transform orders into trades, and communicate the trade information back to the traders and to a central clearing system. From a design perspective a securities market can be thought to consist of two parts; a communication system, and a trading mechanism. Amihud and Mendelson (1990) have used this approach in their proposed ICTS (integrated computerized trading system) market system.

For a market to be perfect, it must be frictionless and infinitely deep and liquid with trading and information freely and instantaneously available to all participants. A perfect market does not restrict the size of a transaction or the creation of innovative securities. In a market with a frictionless trading mechanism, traders do not incur any direct or indirect costs in the trading process itself.

But in a real market, various types of costs are involved in all transactions. In addition to the direct costs of brokers commissions and exchange fees, a trader incurs search costs, information costs, delay costs and market impact costs (Hasbrouck and Schwartz 1988).

Searching for the best price is both costly and time consuming. If the marginal improvement in price is less than the additional cost of the search, the trader will trade at the imperfect price. The delay caused by the search can add additional risk. While the trade is not being made, the price may move in an unfavorable direction. Delays are also caused by the trading mechanism since orders are not instantly transformed into trades. By the time an order is executed it may be suboptimal for it to do so. The price differential in execution of stale orders is borne by the investors. The risk of execution delays and information delays are amplified by short term (intraday) market volatility, a variable that can be controlled by market design (Osborne 1965).

Market impact costs result from the fact that markets are not infinitely deep or liquid. A large buy or sell order may have to be fragmented into different transactions or even routed to other markets and traded at different prices. If the market is not deep (i.e. if it is thin) then the execution of the first portions of the large order will adversely affect the remainder. The bid-ask spread is a measure of the cost of illiquidity. A market is deep and liquid when a large number of orders (market orders, quotes, limit orders) are available with the bid and ask prices close to each other.

The efficient market hypothesis (EMH) is built on the ability of the market to collect, aggregate, and disseminate information (Fama 1965). Individual participants bring certain bits of information to the market. The market combines and aggregates these bits of data into a market consensus. This consensus is revealed through the clearing price and disseminated to all traders. As such the market price summarizes and validates all the information brought to the market by the traders and provides useful information to the economy as a whole. An excellent analysis of the information content of prices has been performed by Garbade, Pomrenze, and Silber (1977) and experimentally tested by Plott (1986).

In reality, the available communication technology as well as the market design and structure determine the extent to which a market can fulfill this role. A participant may enter the market with his own assessment of the true value of a security but once in the market he derives information from the quoted prices of other traders. As a result he revises his expectations. The traders thus learn by observing each other's prices and quickly come to a consensus. The process of price discovery is supported by the communication system of the market. Its rapidity and efficiency is determined by the structure and design of the system.

The usual gauge of market quality is its liquidity with the added requirement of low volatility (Amihud and Mendelson 1987). A market is liquid when it has a sufficiently large number of securities and participants so that any one of them can trade near the equilibrium value of the asset. In addition to being deep and liquid, a well designed market must contain a trading mechanism that process orders, and transform orders into trades without delay and in a smooth and orderly manner.

In the late '70s, there was a great deal of interest in the newly legislated National Market System, or NMS. In 1977, the NYSE was considering the establishment of the CLOB (consolidated limit order book) as part of a move toward an electronic market. The CLOB, as described by Peake, Mendelson, and Williams (1989) 'opens' the limit order book. It was felt that by revealing limit orders to the trading public the market would be made more efficient and achieve a more optimal asset allocation. More important, to design the electronic markets of the future, the market architecture had to be re-thought and the role of the dealers and the designated specialists were called into question. But while the NASDAQ and some of the regional exchanges converted to radical new market designs based on floorless 'screen trading', the NYSE continued to rely on the specialist system and saw automation only as a way to make the specialist based trading mechanism more efficient.

THE MICROSTRUCTURE OF THE NYSE

In the Walrasian market of economic theory (Walras 1874), each participant arrives with a basket of goods and a well defined utility function. Trading begins with a random set of prices that are posted by an 'invisible hand' to which each trader bids or offers the desired quantities of goods. The invisible hand then uses these prices and quantities to draw the supply and demand curves and to determine their intersection through a process of 'tatonnement' which defines the single Pareto optimal price at which all market orders will clear. This description applies to the Walrasian market as modified by Edgeworth (1988) to allow for recontracting so that no trade actually occurs during the price discovery process. All trades are deferred until the clearing equilibrium price has been 'discovered'. The tatonnement process requires that no new information arrive during price discovery and the participants maintain a constant set of utility curves and expectations.

Baumol (1965) contrasts the Walrasian market with the NYSE pointing out two significant ways in which they differ. First, the NYSE does not depend on the invisible hand but assigns a market maker called the 'specialist' to operate the market. Second, the Walrasian market is a 'call' market in that it aggregates buy and sell orders to determine the clearing price and then 'calls' the market at the that price; while the NYSE is a continuous market except for the opening each day (in which it is a call market). The important property of the continuous market is that matching orders may not always exist for orders as they arrive. Such a market has the potential of becoming unstable with wide price fluctuations unless a stabilizing 'reservoir' is available to soak up the imbalance in the order flow. When the price is affected by the trading mechanism in this manner, it is no longer an unbiased estimator of true value as the EMH requires but is biased by an amount that is attributable to the market design.

At the NYSE, such a 'reservoir' is effected not only by the specialist's limit order book but by the specialist himself who buys and sells on his own account to fulfill his duty of maintaining a "fair and orderly market" while at the same time providing a high degree of liquidity to investors by converting orders into trades quickly and at a price close to that at the the last trade.

Each of over 4,000 stocks traded in the New York Stock Exchange is assigned to one of 59 specialist firms that act as market makers. The NYSE is, in a sense, an aggregate of 59 markets assembled on a single floor and operating under a uniform set of trading rules. Each one of these mini markets is self contained in one of the kiosks distributed throughout the floor and known as "specialist's posts". It is in these kiosks that the specialist operates the market and maintains the limit order book for the stocks assigned to him.

Along the walls of the NYSE floor are a series of cubicles that serve as offices for the floor traders and brokers. These brokers represent member firms on the floor and process orders forwarded to them by the retail brokers. Each member firm may have several floor brokers each assigned a specific group of stocks. The broker's cubicle is located so that it is as near as possible to the specialist posts which handle his stocks.

A typical order for a stock may proceed as follows: An individual investor contacts his (retail) broker and places an order. The retail broker may combine the order with other orders he holds and then calls his floor trader assigned to that stock and conveys the total interest in the stock. The floor trader may further aggregate orders. He then walks over to the specialist's post where the stock is being traded. If it is a market order, he either consummates the trade at the specialist's quoted price, or negotiates a trade at a better price. The other side of the trade is one or more limit orders in the specialist's book or the specialist himself who may choose to participate as a dealer. If it is a limit order outside the currently quoted bid and ask prices of the specialist, the broker leaves the order with the specialist who enters it into his limit order book.

A market order is one which specifies the quantity to buy or sell but does not specify price. It is expected that the order will be processed at the prevailing "market price". The investor placing a market order is almost assured that the trade will be carried out within minutes of his order and therefore does not assume any liquidity risk. However, the price may vary usually over a range of 1/4 of a dollar or more depending on the price volatility of the market for the stock. The investor is therefore subject to 'price risk' and this risk increases with price volatility.

A limit order, on the other hand, specifies both the number of shares and the price at which the transaction is to be made. Since the price is predetermined, price risk is eliminated. However, the investor faces 'liquidity risk' since he is not guaranteed that the trade will occur. Limit orders provide liquidity to the market since they form a ready reservoir of buy and sell commitments against which market orders can be executed. In addition, since there are usually limit orders at each 1/8th increment of price, they form a barrier to price movements and thereby dampen price fluctuations. The limit order 'book' thus plays a key role in market quality and its proper management is an essential function of the specialist.

The role of price volatility is complex (Amihud and Mendelson 1987). Although it obviously increases the price risk of market orders, it decreases the liquidity risk of limit orders. Simulation tests by Hakansson, Beja, and Kale (1985) show that the depth of the limit orders dampens short term volatility for a given level of informational volatility. Alternately, for the same depth of limit orders, increased informational volatility increases short term volatility. These relationships are strongly controlled by the ratio of market orders to limit orders. Stoll (1985) reports that more than 60% of the orders at the NYSE are market orders.

THE "ELECTRONIC DISPLAY BOOK" TECHNOLOGY

Until recently, the limit order book was indeed a notebook about 4 inches wide and 11 inches high. The specialist kept these books, one for each stock in his market, up on a shelf in his post. If a limit order came in, he would pull down the book and enter the order. He would frequently review the book to update his quoted prices (the bid and ask) or to execute matching orders in the proper time and price priority. Lower asking prices are given priority over higher asking prices. Higher bid prices are given priority over lower bids. Multiple orders at the same price are processed on a first come first served basis. Small market orders are usually completed at the quoted prices while larger market orders soak deeper into the limit orders and the specialist's account and require complex price computation and negotiation procedures.

In recognition of the importance of limit order book management to the maintenance of a 'fair and orderly market', beginning in 1983, the SIAC (Securities Industry Automation Corporation) began the development of an 'Electronic Book' to replace the paper and pencil book used by the specialists. The SIAC is jointly owned by the NYSE and the American Stock Exchange (Amex) and serves as the IT arm of both firms. The Electronic Book is a micro-computer system that is connected through a high speed LAN to the firm's Tandem computers in Brooklyn. The Tandems are in turn linked via satellite to order entry terminals at retail brokerage offices nationwide. In this system, orders, especially limit orders, need not be called into the floor brokers for delivery to the specialist. Retail brokers nationwide may enter orders directly into the system which automatically routes the order to the post of the specialist who handles the stock.

The book for one to six stocks may be displayed on each screen. A separate 'window' is used for each stock. Each of these windows displays the limit orders in proper price sequence with the lowest ask and the highest bid being innermost. These prices are used by the specialist to determine his own quotes that are to be posted outside the kiosk. Orders at the same price are arranged in time sequence. Matching orders are indicated by flashing highlighted bars and executed when a clerk at the post touches the 'execute' button. When an order arrives electronically, it is routed into the appropriate window. The window flashes temporarily to alert the clerk that a new order has arrived. The order is then prioritized by price and time and entered into the Electronic Book.

The system has properties of an on-line order entry system as well as those of decision support. The OLTP (On Line Transaction Processing) portion of the system delivers order information to the post more efficiently than the method involving the linkage via the floor broker. The decision support aspects of the system are those that assist the specialist in maintaining price-time priority, determining when matching orders may be executed, and aggregating limit orders to process large market orders.

When the system was ready for pilot scale implementation, the specialists were less than eager to participate. The information in the book is considered by the specialists to be confidential and sensitive. In some ways, it represents "inside information" to which only the specialist is privy and which can be used by the specialist to trade on his own account for a profit. They feared that the Electronic Book would leak out this information. However, the crash of October 19, 1987 convinced most specialists that they would not be able to cope with a high trading volumes without the Electronic Book and by December 1989 more than 1500 stocks had been converted.

The Electronic Book, in conjunction with the DOT order routing system, contains properties of both a communication system and a trading mechanism. As a communication tool, it speeds up order transmission to the specialist's book and return of trade data back to the off-floor traders. This process makes the exchange and the limit order book directly accessible to a much larger population and allows faster communication of orders and trade information. In addition, the system also affects the trading mechanism by automatically sorting, matching, and executing orders and updating the book. The specialist is able to directly maintain a much larger list of limit orders. Therefore, a larger number of limit orders directly participate in price formation. Finally, order execution is faster. It is therefore reasonable to expect that the Electronic Book will affect liquidity and price volatility at the transactional or intraday level.

THE PRICE FORMATION PROCESS

Price formation in the specialist market has been studied by Osborne (1965), Osborne and Niederhoffer (1966), Granger and Morgenstern (1970), Barnea (1974), Beja and Goldman (1977), Hakansson, Beja, and Kale (1985), Stoll (1985), and Amihud and Mendelson (1988). Most of the models are based on the analysis of Osborne (1965) in which he postulated that at the transactional level (tick to tick) prices are formed by a well defined "interaction between limit orders and market orders". A "tick" is 1/8th of a dollar. It is the smallest amount by which stock prices may move at the NYSE.

In an analysis of the Fitch data on individual transactions, Osborne and Niederhoffer (1965) found that although close to close price movements followed a random walk process as postulated by the theory of efficient markets, movement of prices from transaction to transaction did not. They discovered patterns in intraday prices that showed that consecutive price changes were negatively correlated, that is, a rise is more likely to be followed by a fall than by another rise; that prices at even eighths (0, 1/4, 1/2, 3/4) were 'sticky', that is, consecutive trades at the same price are more likely to occur at even eighths than at odd eighths; that a large change is more likely to be followed by a large correction than a small one; and that prices behaved as if changes of 0 had not occurred.

These observations led Osborne to conclude that intraday price movements were "the natural consequence of the mechanics of trading". These 'mechanics' consist of interactions between market orders and limit orders. According to Stoll (1985), a majority of the orders at the NYSE are market orders. These are orders that seek maximum liquidity by being executed quickly at the prevailing market price or 'better' (lower for buy orders, higher for sell orders). The speed of execution of these orders and the determination of the price at which they are consummated   are important steps in the trading mechanism that determines market quality and intraday price behavior.

Market orders are executed against limit orders and against the specialist's own inventory at the quoted price of the specialist. The specialist not only makes his commission on such orders but may also turn a profit in the deal. If the specialist 'quotes his book', he offers to transact the market order immediately at the best limit order (lowest sell order or highest buy order) in his limit order book. The quoted bid and ask prices differ by the so called bid-ask spread. This means that a transaction at the same point in time can occur at two different prices separated by the spread depending on whether the market order is buy or sell. This double price feature and the restriction of minimum price movements to 1/8 explain some of Osborne's findings. (The 1/8 price rule is historical and goes back to the Spanish gold piece which was physically divisible into 8 pieces.)

Another important characteristic of the market mechanics that affects intraday price movements is that it is a continuous market with 'random' order arrivals which may cause temporary and random order imbalances. An order imbalance occurs when there are more buy orders than sell orders or vice versa so that they cannot all be converted to trades without some intervention. If order arrival is truly random with equal frequencies of buy and sell orders, then no imbalance occurs. The limit orders prevent price movements by more than the spread in either direction. This explains the pattern of reversals (negative serial correlation). When order imbalances occur, they will soak deeper into the limit orders and the price movements will show a continuation.

In Osborne (1965) these trading mechanics have been encapsulated into a differential equation. Though this model is based on extremely simplifying assumptions (for example, it ignores the specialist's inventory) and is empirically untested, it does formalize the interaction mechanism between limit and market orders and it does predict observed patterns in intraday price movements.

The important conclusion from the works of Osborne and Niederhoffer (1966) and Granger and Morgenstern (1970) is that the intraday price volatility contains a variability induced by the trading mechanism. This idea was used by Barnea (1974) to build an objective criterion for evaluating the performance of specialists. He argued that 'good' specialists ought to be able to keep the market relatively frictionless and minimize the market generated volatility. He proposed that price volatility at the transaction level consists of two components - that which is generated by the market mechanics or the so called 'specialist effect', and that which is generated by external information and noise or what he calls the 'informational effect'.

Barnea reasoned that the performance of specialists can be gauged by by a ratio of variances. If this ratio is defined as intraday variance over interday variance then ratios close to unity would indicate 'good' specialist performance and high ratios would be symptomatic of bad performance. Since ratios of variances ought to be F-distributed, he felt that observed differences in this ratio could be statistically tested. This approach and his attempt to make an empirical test suffered from some shortcomings which he acknowledged.

First, a ratio of variances is F-distributed only if they are independent. In Barnea's case, the two variances were highly correlated since one was a component of the other. A more serious problem was that Barnea did not have access to intraday data but attempted to test his theory anyway by arguing, somewhat ineffectively, that the notion could be applied to 'short term' and 'long term' volatility in general and that the precise definition of short and long term was somewhat arbitrary.

In his empirical test he used interday variability as being 'short term' and a 9-day period as being 'long term'. The test failed because many of his performance ratios turned out to be less than one - an impossibility in his theoretical model. Along with the generally known fact that interday price movements follow the random walk (Fama 1965) and the well documented informational content of interday movements by event studies (Brown and Warner 1985), these findings by Barnea provide additional evidence that interday variability of prices largely reflect information and informational noise.

A similar model of price formation at the transaction level by Beja and Goldman (1977), Hasbrouck and Schwartz (1988), and Hakansson, Beja, and Kale (1985) also imply allocation of volatility to market mechanics and information. The model proposed by Beja in differential equation form as well as its difference equation version (Amihud and Mendelson 1989) require knowledge of the ex ante "intrinsic value" of the stock rather than an a priori definition of what constitutes 'short term' and 'long term'. However, the difference is only superficial. Using the daily close prices as 'intrinsic' value when studying transaction prices is equivalent to defining daily movements as long term and transactional movements as short term. Similarly, the proposition by Hasbrouck and Schwartz (1988) that long term (interday) returns ought to be a product of short term (they used half hour intervals) returns under ideal market conditions is once again a re-statement of Barnea's model of market quality. The literature therefore shows some consensus that the intraday price volatility contains a component that can be ascribed to the 'rust' (Baumol 1965) in the machinery responsible for price formation.

EMPIRICAL TEST

We wish to discover whether the switch to the electronic book has affected the operation of the market mechanics. If it has, it should affect that aspect of prices behavior that is sensitive to market mechanisms. It is proposed, in light of the arguments made above, that the intraday variability of prices is an appropriate measure of the response of the market to changes in mechanism. One measure of variability is the range. Therefore the diurnal range of prices - adjusted for the net absolute interday change, trading volume, and average price is chosen as the response variable for this study. Referring to this value as the 'excess intraday volatility', the hypothesis to be tested can be stated as Ho: The excess intraday volatility has not been affected by the implementation of the Electronic Book; or, the adjusted intraday volatility after implementation of electronic trading is the same as that before implementation; against Ha: The excess intraday volatility after implementation of electronic trading is not the same as that before implementation.

The principal limitation of the empirical tests arises from the inability of the researcher to randomly assign 'subjects' (stocks) to 'treatments' (conversion to electronic trading). The conversion schedule over time was a given and best efforts are made to remove confounding effects using statistical means. Further, since the study limits itself to a single exchange and a single technology, direct generalization of all aspects of the findings may not be possible. However, using extant theories of market mechanism, implications may be drawn that may be applied to other exchanges and automation methods.

Market Microstructure and the Impact of Information Technology: Previous Research

This section is a summary of previous research into the impact of information systems and that of market microstructure and exchange automation. Until recently, information systems researchers did not specifically address impact and effectiveness issues with respect to exchange automation and researchers in finance noted the effects of electronic trading only in the normative based on presumed impacts on price volatility and market quality. Recently the research team of Yakov Amihud (Finance, NYU) and Haim Mendelson (MIS, Stanford) has made significant contributions in this field. Their interdisciplinary papers offer new insights into market automation issues and have served to catalyze this line of inquiry by researchers in both Finance and MIS. Such studies have taken on a new importance and urgency after the market break of October 1987 even as the conversion to electronic trading proceeds unchecked and raises many unanswered question for market designers and regulators. This chapter presents the current study in light of these developments and places the work in the perspective of the overall research agenda not only in market automation but in the study of the impact of information systems in general. It begins by presenting the foundation research on MIS impact and the extension possible by using the newly proposed scientific case study methodology. Relevant research on market microstructure and trading mechanism is then described with respect to the type of information systems to be studied. Finally, the focus shifts to papers on exchange automation and a distillation of these findings that are to be applied in this work.

THE IMPACT OF INFORMATION SYSTEMS

Munshi (1991) presents a meta study of MIS effectiveness research which shows that this line of inquiry has proceeded along several disparate but complementary avenues. The avenues differ according to the social paradigm of the firm, the method of measurement, and the scope of the study that each researcher has chosen to use. In this framework, the present study belongs to a class of MIS research that views the firm in terms of rational objectivism and seeks to detect the impact of IT in terms of rational measures of performance of the enterprise. The measurement method used in such research is direct observation of rational indices of business performance rather than opinion surveys of users or managers. This philosophy holds that the impact of information systems will reveal itself in the output of the enterprise (Weill and Olson 1989). The output of a market is the price. Therefore the price behavior of the market is examined to detect the impact of information technology.

An early work along these lines is that of Lucas (1975). In a field setting, the author made direct observations of the performance of sales agents who were using a 'Sales Information System' (SIS). Although survey research methods were used to assess system usage, 'decision style', and attitudes, the performance of the sales agents was measured with "total dollar bookings" - an objective measure that could be directly observed. The primary independent variable was the user's reported usage of the system. Other determinants of performance were used as control variables. Lucas found a significant correlation of performance with reported usage in some divisions but not in others. The Lucas study could have been improved if a research design were used in which the implementation of the SIS were made one division at a time and both longitudinal and cross sectional comparisons of performance were possible as is the case in the present work.

King and Rodriguez (1978) used a laboratory setting to obtaining objective measures of performance to evaluate the impact of a computer program called 'SICIS' or Strategic Issue Competitive Information System. The purpose of SICIS is to 'aid managers in resolving competitor-related strategic issues'. Two groups of MBA students were asked to solve a simulated business problem. The treatment group was allowed to use the SICIS program while a control group used manual methods. The students' solutions were graded by professors and these grades were used as measures of performance. The study was inconclusive.

In the 1980s many researchers proposed using economics and accounting as the reference disciplines on which to base measures of IT impact at the firm level. Cron and Sobol (1983) attempted to detect the impact of IT penetration on broad measures of profitability and growth. They used accounting ratios such as ROI (return on investment) as the dependent variables and the extent of IT deployed as the independent variables in a large cross sectional study within a single industry (wholesale companies). Their results were not statistically significant possibly due to the existence of more powerful determinants of financial success that were not controlled.

A similar cross sectional study by Stabell (1983) attempted to relate IT investment and penetration to the efficiency with which the firm transforms inputs to outputs. The efficiency is measured using 'frontier analysis'. In this procedure, production data of the firm are used to compute the parameters of a production function such as the Cobb-Douglas ($Q = Q_0 * L^a K^{(1-a)}$). These functions are, of course, dependent on the 'technology' used in the production in a microeconomic sense. Stabell's hypothesis is that information technology also affects the production function parameters and it is in the changes of these parameters that the impact of IT is revealed. However, the empirical study was inconclusive. In my view, production functions and accounting ratios are too far removed from the outputs that are directly affected by IT. Other variables that are more important cannot easily be controlled in cross sectional studies.

But researchers continue to look for relationships between IT expenditure and overall firm performance. Chismar and Kriebel (1985) attempted to improve the power of these tests by selecting a homogeneous group of 19 firms within a single industry classification from the Compustat database. Their paper is very scholarly and provides great insight into the problems of measuring the impact of IT but their results are disappointing. "There is no clear relationship between the level of IS expenditure ... and performance", they conclude.

Strassman (1982, 1984, 1985) argued that information technology (IT) added value to the firm and that this value ought to be measurable. He divided the business enterprise into 'management' and 'operations' and sought to define the determinants of management productivity and management value and to determine how these variables are affected when information technology is deployed. Although these arguments are "compelling" (Chismar and Kriebel 1985), they do not lead to unambiguous testable implications.

On average firms spend around 2% of their budget on IT. But this figure varies greatly from one industry to another. Some researchers reasoned that the cross sectional tests would be more successful in industries that are more IT intensive. The insurance industry, a large investor in information technology, was studied by Bender (1986) and Harris and Katz (1988). Both sought a correlation between total investment in IT and overall firm performance. Bender found that an investment of 15-20% of assets into IT was optimal for insurance companies. Firms that spent more than this or less did not perform as well. He also found that investment in software was not correlated with performance. Both his findings may have to do with differences in software development and maintenance and overall efficiency in utilizing IT as pointed out by Weill nd Olson (1989).

The Harris and Katz (1988) study found that IT investment by insurance companies averaged 14% of assets and that a positive correlation existed between investment in IT and overall firm performance (ROI). However, causality may not be inferred since firms that earn a higher ROI due to other causes may have more funds available for investment in IT. A similar study of the banking industry, another big spender in IT, by Turner (1985) found that banks held, on average, 5.2% of their assets in IT but no relationship existed between overall performance and the IT investment.

Floyd and Wooldridge (1990) ascribe the failure of past research to their lack of control for strategic variables. They offer a contingency model in which the effect of the adoption of information technology is measured only after the effect of the 'competitive strategy' of the firm has been considered. Other variables are also controlled and the study is restricted to a single industry. To further increase precision, IT investment is classified into 'Product' oriented systems such as automated teller machines and 'Process' oriented systems such as decision support systems. In a sample of 130 banks, they found that performance, measured as the ROI, was directly affected by 'product IT' and inversely affected by 'process IT'. The direct effect was statistically significant at the 10% level while the inverse effect was not found to be significant. The model, including IT variables, and strategic variables, explained 13.6% of the total variance in ROI. Although the findings are weak, they represent the first successful study of this nature and show that these studies are improved when specific technologies are targeted and when other variables are statistically controlled.

The contingency approach of Floyd and Wooldridge (1990) is similar to that used in PIMS (1984). In the PIMS study, firms were categorized with respect to their 'strategic position'. 'Contingency Theory' is essentially a statement that an interaction exists between two explanatory variables, i.e., the effect of t1 depends on the level of t2. The PIMS study found an interaction between strategic position and IT investment. Firms with a strong strategic position are more likely to benefit from IT investment. Firms with a weak strategic position show a lower correlation between IT investment and firm performance.

Crowston and Treacy (1986) proposed various alternate economic measures of IT effectiveness but there has been no follow-up empirical work along these lines. Bakos (1987) decried complete reliance on economic and accounting variables and suggested other dependent variables such as organizational structure and competitiveness. Munshi (1991) extends the work of Bakos and argues that the power of the statistical tests on global economic variables is low because of the relatively weak effect of IT. The power can be improved by targeting those dependent variables that are expected to be directly affected by the specific type of IT implementation being tested.

Munshi (1994) uses this strategy to evaluate the impact of IT in the retail merchandising industry. Rather than total IS investment and penetration the study targets specific technologies whose adoption can be related to a reduction in inventory. The independent variable is the extent of diffusion of these specific technologies. The dependent variable used is the level of inventory rather than overall profitability since the latter would be affected by sales, financing decisions, and macro economic factors. The study finds that inventory as a percent of sales, controlled for prevailing inflation and interest rates, has not gone down even with extensive deployment of POS terminals and automated inventory and purchasing systems. These findings challenge conventional assumptions about the impact of such innovations.

In a 'case study' of five manufacturing firms Weill and Olson (1989) found that firms track IT investment differently and therefore these numbers may not be comparable in cross sectional studies. They also found that 'political considerations' were important in IT investment decisions and that managers used industry average investment as a guide. By performing an in depth study of a few firms instead of a large cross sectional study, the Weill and Olson study was able to gain new insights that had eluded previous researchers.

THE CASE STUDY METHODOLOGY

The proposition by Benbasat (1987) and Allen (1989) that a properly designed case study can be a legitimate form of scientific inquiry is a significant development in business research and has important implications for the study of IT impact. Conventional research methods using large statistical samples throw together widely different systems under the rubric of 'information technology' whose expected impact cannot be easily defined or measured. The sampling process also amalgamates many firms that may differ in their competitive strategy (Floyd and Wooldridge 1990) or their ability to utilize the technology (Weill and Olson 1989). The statistical sample is justified by the notion that in a truly random sample, such nuances will tend to cancel each other out. But truly random samples are seldom used in practice and the 'canceling' process creates a high residual variance that reduces the chances of detecting real effects of information technology.

The exemplary case study of Markus (1983) shows that a detailed and careful investigation of a single implementation can result in significant new knowledge and understanding about the nature of IT's impact on the firm. In her famous study of user resistance to IT implementation, Markus first formulates three conflicting theories - that implementation success is determined by (1) properties of the users alone, (2) properties of the system alone, and (3) the interaction between (1) and (2). To test her theories she makes controlled observations of a single implementation and uses 'controlled deductions' that allow for replicability and generalizability.

The deductive process is one of deriving specific testable implications of broader theories which, according to the scientific method, must possess the property of falsifiability. Markus deduced through a series of logical arguments that an implication of the interaction theory is that IS implementation causes a re-distribution of power in the organization. Gainers will accept the system while losers will resist.

Case studies are performed in the field with no intervention by the researcher. Therefore, there is no opportunity to specify research designs a priori. The case study researcher must utilize fortuitous control events that occur naturally. In the case of Markus, it so happened that a manager at the corporate headquarters who had accepted the new system later resisted when he was transferred to a branch office. The interaction theory was thus confirmed without a large sample and without statistical tests.

The present study is comparable. The research design involves an in-depth study of a single technology (the electronic book) in one market (the NYSE). The fortuitous condition is that the implementation was phased over a period of time so that event time methodology can be used to control for historical effects. Arguments are presented from the point of view of market microstructure and trading mechanism and a testable implication is derived - that the impact of electronic trading ought to be evident in short term volatility of prices. Then a statistical test is designed to control for known extraneous and concomitant determinants of volatility and measure the impact of the deployment of electronic trading.

INVESTIGATION OF THE MICROSTRUCTURE OF THE NYSE

Financial theory stresses economic value and market dynamics of the investors but generally ignores the role played by the market mechanics in pricing and price volatility. The theories normally dispense with market mechanism considerations by assuming a perfect and frictionless market of unspecified and inconsequential structure. It is therefore possible that the disagreement between observed and theoretical price movements can be explained in terms of market structure (Goldman and Beja, 1979).

A surprisingly thorough analysis of the NYSE specialist system is presented in the Twentieth Century Fund study (Bernheim 1935). The study presents detailed data on the specialist's function including actual data from a limit order book, statistics on the source of the specialist's earnings, and the manner in which the specialist determines his quotes and processes market orders. This information along with a later government report (SEC 1963) and a monograph by Stoll (1985) provide an inside look into the actual mechanism by which trades occur at the exchange.

These studies describe the specialist's role as both active and passive. In the passive role, he is primarily a manager of the limit order book and a facilitator of market orders - a sort of an 'order entry clerk' that maintains records, matches orders, and executes trades. In the active role, he buys and sells on his own account acting as a reservoir that evens out the temporary and random imbalances in the order flow. He earns a commission on all trades and also stands to make a profit (or loss) when he trades for himself. The SEC (1963) study shows that most of his income is derived from trading.

How is it possible for the specialist to make consistent and persistent profits in an 'efficient market'? The theory of efficient

markets (Fama 1965) would predict that the specialist would lose as
frequently as he would win and that his long run average profit would
be zero. The answer, says Baumol (1965) is that the specialist has
'inside information' or some advantage over other traders. These
advantages are analyzed by Baumol (1965), Osborne (1965),
Niederhoffer and Osborne (1966), Granger and Morgenstern (1970),
Barnea (1974), Goldman and Beja (1979), Stoll (1985), Hakansson,
Beja, and Kale (1985), Mendelson (1987), and Amihud and Mendelson
(1990). The specialist operates as a monopoly, has exclusive knowledge
of the orders in his limit order book, and quotes his market order buy
and sell prices with a differential that always generates a profit. He
works at once as a paid auctioneer (since he is paid commissions) and as
a dealer (since he buys and sells at his quoted prices from his own
inventory).

In his analysis, Baumol (1965) compares the NYSE trading
mechanism to the ideal market design. The ideal market is perfect and
frictionless and efficiently allocates the economy's capital. In the perfect
market, external informational effects and associated noise determine
prices and price fluctuations. The trading mechanism faithfully reflects
these external signals and does not in itself contribute to price behavior.
But the NYSE is not a Walrasian call auction market where the Pareto
optimal price can be determined but a continuous market where order
imbalances may occur; there are not a large number of buyers and
sellers who act as price takers but a small number of floor brokers and
the specialist who can negotiate prices; the order imbalances are
smoothed out and a fair and orderly market is maintained only to the
extent that the specialist is able and willing; the specialist does not
play a purely passive role and does not simply observe the prices that
the market reveals but actually participates in the price formation
process; the specialist has monopoly power in the market for the stocks
assigned to him; the specialist has inside information on the contents
of the limit order book; and trading is not costless but incur direct
transaction costs and market impact costs.

Baumol's analysis shows that these imperfections of the NYSE
specialist system renders the mechanism 'rusty' so that the market
'machinery' itself contributes to price formation at least in the intraday
transaction to transaction movements in price. These 'artificial' market
induced price movements are due partly to the fact that the specialist's
quotes are arbitrary within a range and partly to the fact that the

specialist is an imperfect manager of limit orders and processor of market orders.

Osborne (1965) and Niederhoffer and Osborne (1966) found that although the interday (close to close) price movements were random as predicted by the theory of efficient markets, the intraday prices were not. Their transaction by transaction analysis of the Fitch intraday data shows a high negative serial correlation between price movements of 1/8th, stickiness of even eighths (i.e. the tendency for 0/8, 1/4, 1/2, and 3/4 to persist), and the tendency to continue after two movements in the same direction. These patterns in price data indicate that the intraday price movements are not informationally efficient but have structural properties and are generated at least in part by the mechanism of the market itself.

The authors propose a model for this mechanism in terms of the interactions between market orders and limit orders. More than half of the orders at the NYSE are market orders, that is they are to be executed 'at the market' price. The other side of the trade may consist of one or more limit orders, or other market orders that arrive at the same time, or the specialist himself. In the last case, the specialist acts as a dealer and buys and sells at his quoted prices and makes the spread. However, he himself may then trade against limit orders in his book which only he knows about. His trading strategy is motivated by his charge to even out order imbalances as well as his desire to make a profit.

In their simplified model of the market microstructure, the specialist's active role is ignored and the specialist's post is considered to be a black box into which market orders and limit orders arrive using some stochastic process and interact to produce transaction prices, the output of the black box. In differential equation form, their model can be written as,

$$dp/dt = [dM/dt] / [-dL/dp]$$

where p is price, t is time, M represents market orders, and L represents limit orders. The equation states that the rate of change of price is positively related to the rate of arrival of 'buy' market orders and inversely related to the slope of the supply curve (limit orders to sell). 'Sell' market orders can be considered to be negative 'buy' orders and 'buy' limit orders are similarly negative 'sell' orders. Using simulation, the authors show that the process can produce intraday price behavior that exhibits the mechanical patterns observed in real prices. This leads the authors to conclude that much of the intraday price volatility is generated by the trading mechanism.

The model is extended by Granger and Morgenstern (1970) to include both the passive and active functions of the specialist. They note that in carrying our his duty of maintaining a fair and orderly market and executing market orders quickly at near the price of the most recent transaction, "the specialist ...becomes a major factor in the price making process" and that at the intraday level of price formation, "the interaction between the two types of orders and the autonomous actions of the specialist will be the major components" of price discovery. Limit orders as well as the specialists inventory (and his willingness to trade) impart liquidity by providing barriers to price movements when executing market orders. The authors feel that the secrecy of the limit order book gives 'special privileges' to the specialist and is an impediment to free and efficient markets. The authors contend that while "daily, weekly, and monthly changes are dominated by a process that produces the random walk", intraday transactional price movements are "dominated by the interaction between the random sequence of market orders and the temporary barriers produced by limit orders".

The idea of attributing short term and long term price volatilities to different processes is further developed and empirically tested by Barnea (1974) who was primarily concerned with developing evaluation criteria for specialist performance. He argues that in the course of fulfilling his role of transforming orders into trades and absorbing order imbalances, the specialist affects price behavior in the short term but not in the long term since order imbalances are 'temporary'.

Demsetz (1968) had also addressed specialist evaluation methods and had suggested that the bid-ask spread, a measure of market illiquidity, should be the proper measure. Barnea points out that Demsetz's illiquidity measure is inadequate because "for an investor selling when a temporary excess of supply exists in the market the size of the spread is of no relevance. For him the important activity of the specialist is the extent to which the specialist reduces his bid price because of the temporary order imbalance". Some specialists are able to keep the market more stable than others and the appropriate measure of specialist performance, that he calls the 'specialist effect', is the price volatility induced by the specialist's activity.

Applying the logic used by Osborne (1965) and Granger and Morgenstern (1970), Barnea (1974) explains that total 'short term' price volatility consists of a 'specialist effect' and an 'informational effect'. The specialist effect does not persist so that in the 'long term' only the informational effect remains. Therefore, he contends, the proper index of specialist performance is the ratio of short term volatility to long term volatility. The same argument can be applied to the market mechanism in general. If the market is perfect and frictionless then Barnea's ratio will be unity and as it departs from the ideal and collects Baumolian 'rust', then the mechanism induces short term volatility and the Barnea ratio rises.

Since Barnea did not have access to intraday data, he attempted to test his theory by using interday price volatility as a short term measure and interweek volatility as a long term measure. The test failed because many of his ratios were less than one - an impossibility in his theory. An implication is that temporary order imbalances are not evident in interday prices and a proper measure of the price volatility imposed by the market mechanism is that portion of the intraday volatility that is not explained by interday volatility.

Beja and Hakansson (1977), and Goldman and Beja (1979) have proposed a mathematical model of the market mechanism at the NYSE that includes both both mechanism effects and informational effects. The authors address two fundamental questions of market design. First, what is the role of the market microstructure in price behavior? and second, what is the role of the specialist within this mechanism?

The model utilizes the dual price concept, that is, the concurrent existence of two prices - an unobservable equilibrium true value, W, which follows a random walk, and an observable trading price, P, which is driven by the equilibrium value and subject to market structure. The model is constructed as a set of stochastic differential equations as:

Equilibrium Value $\quad dW(t) = \mu dt + sdy$

Observed Price $\quad dP(t) = a [W(t) - P(t)] dt + sdz$

W is the price that would be observed in the perfect and frictionless market of economic theory where an "invisible hand" assures market clearing price discovery by equating demand and supply at no cost to the traders. It is therefore free of the effects of market architecture and the trading mechanisms being used. The standard random walk equation may be interpreted to state that the changes in W per unit time are normally distributed about a mean value of μ and a standard deviation of s. The term dy represents a Weiner process.

The effect of the market mechanism is to produce the time series P(t) instead of the theoretical value W(t). Changes in P are taken to be distributed normally about the mean value of (a)(W-P) and a standard deviation of s. The terms a, s, and dz, are determined by the architecture of the market and the trading mechanism being utilized.

The error in the price is given by (P-W) and the changes in P are viewed as corrective i.e., an effort to reach the equilibrium value. In an electrical analogy (mine, not theirs), (W-P) represents the voltage or driving force while 1/a can be thought of as the 'impedence' (to price movements). In that sense, 'a' is an important parameter of the trading mechanism since it determines how rapidly prices tend to approach equilibrium value.

The solution of these differential equations yields a non-linear behavior of changes in P. The variance of the changes in P always asymptotically approaches

$$(s^2 - s^2)/a$$

as the time interval is increased. An implication is that the changes in price (not the prices but the changes in price) are serially correlated and the correlation is determined by the value of 'a' and by the sign of the expression above. If the sign is positive, it means that the trading mechanism itself produces more noise than there is in the equilibrium value. This model is consistent with the patterns in intraday prices observed by Osborne and Niederhoffer (1966) and with Barnea's (1974) theory that intraday prices contain a volatility component that is generated by the trading mechanism.

The role of the specialist is evaluated with the mean square error of the price, that is the average value of (P-W) squared. After the market has stabilized, the mean square error will be given by

$$e^2 = [\mu^2/a^2] + [(s^2 + s^2)/(2a)]$$

The first term is inversely proportional to 'a'; the faster the adjustment process (the 'conductance') the closer P will be to W. The conductance can be increased by communication technology or automation of the order processing and execution system and perhaps by financial innovations. The specialist can affect both 'a' and 's' and he attempts to adjust these to fulfill his charge of keeping the market orderly and smooth by matching supply and demand. In terms of the model, therefore, his job is to minimize e^2 by decreasing 's' without unduly decreasing 'a' or in other words, to minimize volatility to the extent that his actions do not unduly reduce liquidity.

This balancing act between volatility and liquidity has been investigated by Amihud and Mendelson (1989). An asset is liquid if it can be converted to cash quickly and with little transaction cost. Transaction costs can be both direct in terms of fees and dealer margins and indirect in terms of market impact costs and delay costs. As noted, the rational and normative function of the exchange is to provide liquidity while at the same time maintaining a 'smooth and orderly market'. The latter condition is normally construed as a requirement that price volatility should be minimized. However, as Amihud and Mendelson (1989) have shown, volatility cannot be eliminated. Volatility is inexorably linked with trading.

Trading causes volatility and volatility causes trading and trading is essential for liquidity. The relationship between volatility and liquidity is shown in Exhibit 2-1. When trading volume taxes the design capacity of the market to process and absorb orders, an excess volatility is added that can be attributed purely to market mechanism and not to trading itself. Proper market design will attempt to minimize this component of the volatility. We can refer to this as the excess volatility due to friction.

However, attempts to decrease volatility below that which is needed for trading to occur will be at the expense of liquidity. Therefore, volatility cannot be minimized but only optimized for a given market size and structure. The NYSE order processing system is designed for a capacity of 450 million shares per day or approximately six transactions per second. On October 19th and 20th of 1987, it was handling over 25 transactions per second (Peake, Mendelson, and Williams 1989). It has been argued by the Brady Commission Report (Brady 1988) and shown mathematically by the Amihud and Mendelson model (1989) that throughput above capacity alone can explain the excess volatility and market failure observed during this period. If this is true, the information processing system and the market mechanism play a key role in the ability of the market to achieve its dual objectives of maintaining a smooth and orderly market while at the same time providing liquidity.

Amihud and Mendelson (1987, 1989) empirically tested the effect of trading mechanism on stock returns by comparing the open to open and close to close prices. The market opening resembles a call market while the closing prices are generated by a continuous market. The authors found that open to open returns show greater volatility. They also found the open to open returns to be farther removed from normality and to be serially correlated. They attribute these dissimilarities to differences in trading mechanism and conclude that "investors correct perceived errors or noise" at the close.

The impact of execution costs on market quality is examined by Hasbrouck and Schwartz (1988). They argue that in the absence of market induced price movements, short term return volatilties would be given by

$$Var\ (Rs) = Var\ (Rl) / p$$

where p is the number of short term periods in the long term period, Rs = the short term returns, Rl = long term returns, and Var stands for variance. For example, if the short term period is defined as one hour and the long term period is one 6-hour day, then p=6. Market imperfections induced by execution costs (both direct and indirect) will increase the variance of short term returns beyond this value. In the manner of Barnea, they define a 'Market Efficiency Coefficient' as the ratio of the expected value of the short term variance in a perfect market to the actual short term variance. Using 1/2 hour as 'short term' and two days as 'long term' they found that the Amex had the highest market quality (0.862) and the NASDAQ/NMS computerized market had the lowest (0.488). The NYSE rated 0.764. The authors attribute deviations of the market efficiency coefficient from unity to execution costs.

RESEARCH ON EXCHANGE AUTOMATION

Garbade and Silber (1978) used a longitudinal design to study the effect of various innovations in communications in the 19th century. They found that the introduction of the telegraph in 1840 significantly reduced the spread between the prices of the same securities traded at the NYSE and at secondary markets in Philadelphia and New Orleans. They also found that the introduction of the transatlantic cable in 1866 reduced price discrepancies between London and New York for bonds that were traded in both markets. The present study is conceived in the spirit and framework of the Garbade and Silber paper and seeks to establish the impact that recent advances in information technology has had on the structure, operation, and performance of securities markets.

The Garbade and Silber methodology was a simple longitudinal study performed around the date of introduction of each technology. For each event, an event window is described before which the technology was not used and after which the technology was fully implemented. Then, a series of prices (in time) before and after the window are compared using a simple t-test. This method can be criticized since it is subject to extraneous effects such as political and economic changes, wars, deployment of other technologies, changes in trading rules and regulatory constraints, and financial innovation.

The liquidity of secondary markets and intermarket systems in the context of information technology is further examined by Garbade and Silber (1979) in a later paper. Contrary to the commonly held notion that trading frequency causes price volatility, the authors argue that the causal direction may in fact be in reverse. In the Garbade and Silber model, volatility is caused by the speed with which new information can be disseminated. When markets are volatile, investors face "liquidity risk" (inability to convert to cash at a given equilibrium price) and try to compensate by seeking to complete transactions more quickly.

Their model also predicts higher volatility with increased market size where size is measured by the number of participants that can actively engage in trading. The effective size of the NYSE was greatly increased in the mid 19th century by the introduction of the telegraph in 1840 and the subsequent implementation of the stock ticker in 1867 and brokers wires in 1873. These communication technologies gave a larger number of participants direct and faster access to the floor. Because of the volatility induced by market size, investors demanded faster access and order execution. As a result, the market abandoned morning and afternoon auctions and converted completely to continuous operation.

Hakansson, Beja, and Kale (1985) have proposed a model for automating the specialist market with a "programmed specialist". They see the specialist's function primarily in 'demand smoothing' or absorbing order imbalances which are assumed to be temporary and random. In a simulated market orders were stochastically generated and demand was smoothed using a set of rules. Based on these results, the authors conjecture whether the demand smoothing function of the

specialist could be replaced with an expert system at a much lower cost
to traders. But the simulated market did not function very well. The
price opened at $10 and closed at $32. Thus the net 'interday' change
was $22. But the 'intraday' swing was $112 as the stock hit a low of
$6 and a high of $118.

In their paper, "Liquidity, Volatility, and Exchange Automation",
Amihud and Mendelson (1988, 1989) propose an Integrated
Computerized Trading System (ICTS). The ICTS is designed to provide
a high degree of liquidity to traders at low cost and low volatility. Its
designers explain that illiquidity and volatility are related but are not the
same and a proper model of these important concepts is necessary for
the design of automated markets. In an obvious reference to circuit
breakers and trading halts, the authors argue that the benefits to
investors of artificial barriers to volatility are questionable since they
also reduce liquidity. "The added cost of illiquidity should be balanced
against the perceived benefits of lower volatility". The authors also
point out that when the exchange mechanism artificially affects prices,
these prices have a lower information content since they "do not fully
reflect all available information". Market efficiency is therefore lower.

In the design of the ICTS special attention is paid to the
management of the limit order book since limit orders are an important
source of depth and liquidity for the market. They propose an 'open'
consolidated limit order book (CLOB) which would be accessible to all
traders not just to the specialist. Investors can electronically enter limit
orders or market order into the system while viewing all other orders
already in the system. The open CLOB described by some as a
'computerized bulletin board' has actually been implemented at the
Cincinnati Stock Exchange but has been attacked by many researchers.

For example, Grossman and Miller (1986) show that the
arrangement discourages investors from placing limit orders. A public
limit order is "a sitting duck" and can be "hit" by more informed
investors. They argue that an open limit order book will have fewer
limit orders and therefore lower liquidity.

Black (1971) was one of the earliest proponents of a completely
computerized exchange. Twenty years ago, he envisioned an automated
market that would go beyond a system to "help the specialist with the
management of his book of limit orders". The computerized 'screen
trading' he envisioned would eliminate the floor, the floor brokers, and
the specialist. Market efficiency and liquidity are the most important

attributes of a well designed market. He sees the role of computers both as a communication device that brings all orders to a single point for comparison and execution and disseminates trade information back to the investors; and as a comparison and record keeping device that can automatically execute orders.

A case study by Clemons and Weber (1989) describes the 'TRADE' computerized trading system used by Barclay's capital market in London. Users are allowed to see only the current market best bid and ask prices and can trade against these limit orders. The authors see the value of the system as a 'competitive weapon'. It gives Barclay's an edge over other large securities houses that also operate their own capital market. In Britain, the securities industry is deregulated to a much greater extent than it is in the US and the London's International Stock Exchange (ISE), which is already floorless, is undergoing a complete overhaul because of deregulation and automated trading.

The ISE was computerized almost overnight in October 1986 in what is called the 'Big Bang'. The Big Bang conversion is the subject of another case study by Clemons and Weber (1990). The authors found evidence that automation gave the ISE a 'competitive advantage' . Order flow was diverted from small continental exchanges to the ISE which offered faster execution, greater liquidity, and lower transaction costs. However, as the TRADE study shows, the complete deregulation and availability of electronic trading has caused alternate markets to form in the larger securities firms. "The industry faces an uncertain future" as a result of automation and deregulation. Automation may have taken place too fast and the design of the automated system may not have been optimal.

In a study similar to the present work, Hamilton (1989) investigated the impact of commission deregulation and the ITS (Intermarket Trading System) on order flow. The ITS is a component of the National Market, or NMS, first instituted in 1978 with gradual conversion of stocks to the intermarket system through the next decade. When a stock is 'converted' to ITS (or it becomes 'ITS eligible'), the best bid and ask prices for the stock at any US exchanges connected by ITS become available to all exchanges. For example if there is a better quote at Boston, the specialist at the NYSE can trade against it. The hypothesis tested by Hamilton is that the ITS has diverted order flow away from the NYSE and to the regional exchanges. The data showed that in fact the order flow to the NYSE has increased since the implementation but this increase was not found to be statistically significant.

Malone, Yates, and Benjamin (1986) propose that "fundamental changes in market structure may result from the increasing use of information technology". Their paper provides an analytic framework within which market automation can be studied. They prophesy that information technology will cause markets to become more integrated and therefore more efficient. This was the vision and philosophy that caused Congress to sanction the NMS in 1972. Although the implementation of the NMS has given rise to deregulation, off-board trading, the NASDAQ automated exchange, and ITS, there is still no empirical evidence of real benefits or impact on markets of automation.

Peake, Mendelson, and Williams (1989) propose a completely automated market that would remove 'deficiencies' in the present capital markets. Deficiencies include: unequal access to the trading floor to different classes of investors, asymmetric information availability of floor prices, and the inefficient manner in which prices for market orders are negotiated. The proposed solution is complete deregulation, total automation, and 24-hour trading. "Markets should stay open at all times". A component of their automated system is the open and consolidated limit order book (CLOB) which is opposed by the specialists and by many researchers. However, it is widely believed that the NYSE is moving toward around the clock trading in a manner proposed by the authors.

EXHIBIT 2-1
Relationship Between Volatility, Liquidity, and Trading

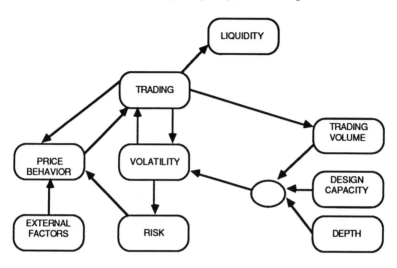

The Empirical Test: Rationale and Methodology

Over the three-year period from 1987 to 1989 several hundred stocks were converted from manual limit order books to the new 'electronic book'. The implementation schedule lists the conversion date, post number, and specialist for each stock that was converted in this period. Daily trade data are available in the CRSP database and include closing prices, diurnal range, and trading volume. The mean absolute diurnal price range is used as a measure of intraday volatility and the net mean absolute daily change is used as an indicator of interday volatility. Intraday volatility is partitioned into a component that varies with interday changes and a component in excess of that which cannot be explained in terms of interday price fluctuations. The excess intraday volatility is the response variable under investigation. We use a longitudinal quasi-experimental design to perform a comparison in 'event time' of the excess volatility before and after the treatment which is expected to cause a step change in the response. The treatment is the implementation of the Electronic Display Book on the floor of the New York Stock Exchange. A linear regression model is used to control for other variables that may also affect excess volatility.

AN EMPIRICAL MODEL OF EXCESS VOLATILITY

The relationship between the measures of variability used in this study is shown in Exhibit 3-1. The intraday price swing is the difference between the day's highest asking price and lowest bid price. It is the range of prices in which the stock traded during the day. Typically, this range is larger than the absolute value of the net change in price at the close and cannot be less than this value. These measures of price variability or volatility are defined as:

Interday(t)   = absolute value of (CLOSE (t) - CLOSE (t-1))
              = a measure of interday variability of prices
Intraday   = (HIGH (t) - LOW (t))
              = a measure of intraday variability of prices
CLOSE (t)   = closing price on day t
HIGH (t)   = highest (asking) intraday price on day t
LOW (t)   = lowest (bid) intraday price on day t

t   = indicates t-th trading day

Following Barnea (1974) we postulate that a portion of the intraday volatility is directly attributable to net interday changes and may therefore be considered to be an economic effect while the remainder is unrelated to the variability of closing prices and may contain information on market microstructure. The total variability may be partitioned into the two components using a linear regression model as follows:

Regression Model
Intraday = a + b1*Interday + b2*Price + b3*Interday*Price + e

Intraday Volatility Ascribed to Economic Effects
b1*Interday + b2*Price + b3*Interday*Price

Excess Intraday Volatility
a + e

The Excess Volatility is the residual intraday price swing which can be considered to be the that portion of 'Intraday' that cannot be explained by the normal economic variables of interday changes and the price level and therefore may be related to trading mechanisms. To test the hypothesis that implementation of electronic trading has affected price behavior, we posit that the excess intraday swing in prices, a + e, adjusted for control variables, will be different after implementation of electronic trading.

The variable PRICE is the mean diurnal price level computed as a simple average between HIGH and LOW;

PRICE = (HIGH + LOW)/2
      = average daily price.

It is expected that the variables Interday and Price will be correlated since economic effects tend to be 'returns-oriented' rather than simply 'price-oriented' (Fama 1965). These colinearities may cause the individual regression coefficients to be unstable since the X'X matrix will approach singularity as its columns become more and more linearly related. However, the intent of this test and the conclusions of this study do not depend on an interpretation of either the sign or the magnitude of these coefficients. Only the residual or 'excess' volatility is subjected to further interpretation and analysis.

DEVELOPMENT OF THE LINEAR MODEL

Three important control variables are identified. These are the specialist, trading volume, and market movement. In quasi-experimental field studies the level of concomitant variables are not experimentally controlled and the value of the response variable must be adjusted for their effect before the that of the treatment may be assessed. For example, it is known that price volatility and trading volume are related. Demsetz (1968), Tauchen and Pitts (1983) and Penman and Ohlson (1985) have found that higher price volatility is associated with higher trading volume. We also deduce from the nature of the specialist's task of managing the limit order book (to reduce order imbalance and provide liquidity) that the impact of the new information system may depend on the level of order flow. We therefore include trading volume as a covariate so that the comparison of excess volatility before and after deployment of the EDB is made after adjustment for differences in mean trading volumes in the two samples.

Barnea (1974) found that the performance of the specialist (his ability to maintain a smooth and orderly market) was affected by whether the price of the stock changed by three ticks (1/8ths of a dollar) or more during the trading day. This effect is consistent with the mechanism by which the specialist absorbs market imbalances and manages the limit order book. As Osborne (1965) and others have noted, price formation in the specialist market is a result of interaction among limit orders, market orders, and the specialists inventory. A 'static' market that is fluctuating about a mean price produces very short term imbalances in both directions that tend to balance each other out with very little effort of the specialist in managing his or her limit order book. However, a market that is 'moving' in one direction or another tends to sustain and even increase the order imbalance. To adjust the excess volatility for this effect, a class variable called 'Market movement' is introduced which can take on two values as follows:

MOVEMENT   =0 if net interday price change < 3 ticks

=1 if net interday price change ≥ 3 ticks

The use of three ticks as a criterion in MARKET MOVEMENT is further supported by research into the quote revision patterns at the NYSE. Jang and Venkatesh (1991) found that quote revision patterns behave differently when the bid-ask spread is three ticks or more. Thus the reasoning presented above, along with the findings of Barnea (1974), Harris (1989), Hasbrouck (1988), and Jang and Venkatesh (1991) endorse the use of this criterion to classify the market into two broad categories as 'moving' and 'static'.

The 'specialist effect' has been noted by Barnea (1974) and Beja and Goldman (1977). The excess intraday volatility is adjusted for this effect by introducing a dummy coding for each specialist;

SPECIALIST   = 0 if it is not this specialist
              = 1 if it is this specialist

There will be as many of these variables as there are specialists who were converted to the electronic system during the period of the test. Approximately 45 specialists were converted. Admittedly, the inclusion of this variable will create a very large X matrix and this may place limits on the types of linear models that are computationally feasible.

Finally, the adjusted excess volatility is tested against the treatment. This is an indicator variable that is used for the mode of trading as:

TRADING METHOD   = 0 stock trading on manual book
                  = 1 electronic book deployed

The adjusted excess volatility is tested against this variable. A significant difference in this measure of intraday price variability will lead to a rejection of the null hypothesis. The full regression model is:

EXCESS = f (VOLUME, MARKET, SPECIALIST, TRADING METHOD)

DATA TO BE EXCLUDED

The market crashed during the week of October 19, 1987 and the week of October 13, 1989. During these periods the market behavior was abnormal and these effects may affect the test of excess volatility. These observations are therefore dropped. Other uncontrolled known external events that may affect the response include new listings, takeovers and mergers, stock buybacks, bankruptcies, lawsuits, new stock issues, stock dividends, and stock splits. Firms which suffered these uncontrolled economic effects around the EDB implementation window are dropped from the sample.

THE VOLATILITY HYPOTHESIS

The research hypothesis is that automation of the specialist's limit order book changes the market microstructure and that this change will be reflected in price behavior. The hypothesis is tested using classical inferential statistics which proceeds as follows. First an explicit null hypothesis is formulated that states that no difference in means exists. Then sample data with and without the EDB treatment are taken and the difference in the sample mean excess volatility is computed.

Then, by making the usual assumptions of homoscedasticity, normality, and correct formulation of the linear model, a probability, 'p-value', is computed. This value represents the chances of realizing the observed difference in means under conditions of the null hypothesis. If the p-value is smaller than a critical number, normally 5%, the data are considered unlikely given the null hypothesis. Since the data were observed, the hypothesis is rejected. The data are then considered sufficient evidence in support of an alternate hypothesis that negates the null. If the probability is larger than the critical value, then the test is inconclusive. Either no difference exists or the power of the test is not sufficient to detect a difference that does exist.

The null hypothesis for the volatility test may be stated as Ho: The adjusted excess intraday volatility has not been affected by the implementation of the Electronic Book; or, the adjusted intraday volatility after implementation of electronic trading is the same as that before implementation. This is negated in the alternate hypothesis as Ha: The conversion to the Electronic Book is associated with a change in excess volatility. The adjusted intraday excess volatility after deployment of electronic trading is not the same as that before deployment.

To test the hypothesisa sample statistic is computed as as SS (treatment) / [SS(error)/n] where SS refers to the sum of squares and n is the error degrees of freedom. The treatment has one degree of freedom. Using the F-distribution, the p-value may be computed. If this probability is sufficiently low (less than 5%) then the null hypothesis is rejected and it is concluded that the implementation of electronic trading is associated with a change in excess intraday volatility of price. If the probability is not sufficiently small, then the null hypothesis may not be rejected and these data are not considered to constitute sufficient evidence that the conversion to electronic trading has affected intraday prices.

The use of the F-distribution to compute these probabilities requires that the residuals be normally distributed and homoscedastic and that the model be correctly formulated. An interpretation of the latter is that external effects that are not in the model may cause the rejection of the null hypothesis. For example, if there exists a general trend in intraday price volatility during the period of the test, then any choice of implementation dates (regardless of whether event time is used or not) will always show a spurious effect. The same sort of spurious result will be obtained if a control variable was missed that caused a large step change in volatility and if a sufficient number of implementation dates were clustered around this phantom intervention.

These concerns need attention only if the null hypothesis is rejected. This is because we wish to support the notion that the effect was that of electronic trading and not spurious; i.e., it is the explicit null hypothesis and not one of the implicit null hypotheses that is to be rejected. We address these concerns by performing an additional inferential test on what we may term the 'incorrect' data. To generate the incorrect data we use the same set of implementation dates but mis-assign them to the list of stocks in the sample. Then as before, we sample volatility and trading volume data around the incorrect implementation dates and apply the same test. If this test results in a rejection of the null hypothesis then it is possible that the rejection in the actual test may have been of an implicit null.

THE LIQUIDITY HYPOTHESIS

Liquidity effects of trading mechanisms have been postulated by Demsetz (1968), Garbade and Silber (1979), Amihud and Mendelson (1990) and others. A test for liquidity effects can be made in a manner similar to the volatility test. In terms of the variables described, liquidity may be defined as the total dollar value of trading in one day per unit of adjusted intraday volatility (after Dubofsky and Groth 1984). In the absence of intraday trade data, the simplifying assumption is made that the simple average PRICE computed as (HIGH+LOW)/2 is a sufficiently good approximation of the weighted average price. The total dollar volume may be approximated as PRICE * VOLUME. The liquidity term is then computed according to the equation

LIQUIDITY = PRICE * VOLUME / INTRADAY

where 'Intraday' is the total intraday range in ticks (1/8ths of a dollar).

This definition of liquidity is an approximation necessitated by data limitations. Had intraday transaction data been available, a more accurate estimate of intraday liquidity could have been computed as the weighted average of the dollar value of each transaction divided by the bid-ask spread at the time that the transaction was made. However, the approximation used does provide useful information and is not expected to introduce any bias in the estimates. The method conforms closely to computations of liquidity used by other researchers (Dubofsky and Groth 1984).

The research hypothesis is that a switch from manual to electronic trading is associated with a change in liquidity. This is formulated into null and alternate hypotheses for inferential testing as Ho: The adjusted liquidity after implementation of electronic trading is the same as that before implementation; against Ha: The adjusted liquidity after implementation of electronic trading is not the same as that before implementation.

The hypothesis is tested using the regression model

LIQUIDITY = f (Market movement, Specialist, Trading)

using a similar statistical procedure as in the test for volatility. Here 'Trading' is the treatment and is either 'manual' or 'EDB'.

DATA ANALYSIS METHODS AND DEFINITIONS

The implementation schedule of the Electronic Book is available from the New York Stock Exchange for the period covering January 1987 to December 1989. For each of over 1200 stocks converted in this period, the schedule lists the date the conversion took place, the post where the equipment was installed and the specialist firm that operates the market for the stock that was converted.

As of April 1987, the database of security prices supplied by the Center for Research on Security Prices (CRSP) contains the daily high (the highest asking price called 'ASKHI' by CRSP), low (the lowest bid price called 'BIDLO' by CRSP), and trading volume (called 'VOL' by CRSP) data in addition to the closing price (or 'PRC'). The intraday volatility variable is computed as

Intraday = ASKHI - BIDLO

and the net interday volatility is measured as

NET = ABS(PRC(J) - PRC(J-1))

where ABS indicates the absolute value and J indicates the jth day in time.

To avoid historical effects, all calendar dates are collapsed into a single event-time framework as described by Brown and Warner (1980, 1985). The time scale is depicted in Exhibit 3-2. All conversion dates are set to time zero and data are collected for the twenty trading days immediately preceding (there are approximately twenty trading days per month). The variable 'Trading' is set to 0 in this window to indicate that the Electronic Book has not been implemented. The twenty trading days immediately following the conversion are skipped to allow time for the specialist to learn to use the new system and to gradually wean himself/herself from the manual book. Data are again collected for a 20-day period from conversion+20 days to Conversion+40 days. For these observations, the categorical variable 'Trading' is set to 1 to indicate that trading using the Electronic Display Book.

Regression analysis is used in this study to make inferences about the 'treatment means' of the response variables 'Excess' and 'Liquidity'. The dichotomous treatment is 'Trading' which takes on the values of 0 or 1. However, because the data are from a field experiment (i.e., a 'quasi-experimental design') other variables that affect the response have not been held constant or experimentally controlled in any way. Therefore a direct comparison of the treatment means is not made. Group means of the response variables are adjusted to correspond to common values of the control variables. An added benefit of including these as control variables in the model is that the variation (sum of squares) in the response variables associated with them is removed from what is considered to be the error sum of squares. The model is closer to 'correct' and the power of the inferential tests is increased.

An assumption of the linear adjustment procedure is that the marginal effect of the covariate on the response variable is independent of the value of the treatment variable. In other words, the regression line of 'Excess' against Trading volume, for example, for Trading='manual' would differ from that of Trading='EDB' only in the value of the intercept term but would have a common slope. It is in fact the difference in the intercepts that is the magnitude of the 'effect' of the treatment on the response. Although the regression procedure is fairly robust to heterogeneity of slopes, it is necessary to perform a check to ascertain that the principle of parallelism is not grossly violated.

The check for parallelism is made as a preliminary step prior to using the regression model by including appropriate interaction terms. For instance, in the linear model for 'Excess', an interaction term Trading*Volume is included at the end of the variable list and the sequential sum of squares for the interaction (trading volume*trading method) is interpreted as the additional sum of squares due to the difference in the slope of the regression line in the two regions. The F-distribution is then used to assess whether the interaction observed in the sample is evidence of real interactions extant in the population from which the sample was drawn.

In analysis-of-variance terminology the independent variable is called the 'treatment' (if there is more than one, they are called 'factors'). In this case, the treatment variable is 'Trading method'. It has two levels or 'treatment groups' which are mutually exclusive and which, between them, contain all the observations. Some of the control variables are categorical. These categorical variables are included because their level could not be controlled in the field and it is suspected that their level affects the response variable independent of the treatment. Their inclusion reduces the error sum of squares and creates homogeneous blocks within which the level of these variables are constant and the effect of the treatment can be more clearly observed.

However, the interactions need to be checked first to determine whether their effects are uniform in the two treatment groups. Since the observations were not randomly assigned to the blocks they are not balanced in that the treatment groups may have different sample sizes. Further, some of the blocks may be empty. The computation of sum of squares requires appropriate weights to overcome the biasing effects of the unbalance (difference in sample size).

The comparison of treatment means are made after they have been adjusted for the concomitant variables. The adjusted treatment means are referred to as 'least square means'. For example, in the 'Excess volatility' model, the least square mean adjusted for VOLUME would be given by

$$\text{ls } \mu \text{ (Excess}_i) = \mu \text{ (Excess}_i) - \text{ß2} * (\mu(\text{Excess}_i) - \mu(\text{Volume}))$$

where i represents the i-th treatment group (in this case either Trading=0 or Trading=1) and μ represents the mean. This adjustment is equivalent to making the comparison of the response at the same (average) value of the control variable.

The deployment of the Electronic Display Book for each stock in the NYSE may be considered an 'intervention' in a time series of volatility data. According to the research hypothesis, we would expect to see a step change in the response as a result of the intervention. If the data are indeed a time series they may not be independent as is assumed in a regression model but may have autoregressive (AR) or moving average (MA) properties. Intervention analysis methods described by Box and Tiao (1976) and Cook and Campbell (1979) would then be applicable and could be used to remove any ARMA processes in the time series and test the residual 'white noise' (independent data) for evidence of a step change.

The methodology allows for a generalized transfer function rather than the step function hypothesized in this case. The series is first examined for ARIMA (auto regressive integrated moving average) processes by plotting a correlogram along with partial autocorrelations and inverse autocorrelations. Based on the sample autocorrelation properties the appropriate ARIMA process is formulated and removed from the series leaving a white noise residuals that are unrelated to each other and therefore may be treated as independent in the further linear analysis.

In the intervention methodology the further linear analysis consists of cross correlations with covariates and the treatment or 'intervention' which are formulated to correspond to the hypothesized transfer function. The absolute value of the regression weight for the transfer function $|b|_t$ is then tested using the statistical hypotheses as Ho: $|b|_t = 0$; or, there is no impact of the intervention in this form of the transfer function against Ha: $|b|_{t>0}$; or, the intervention is associated with a change in the time series.

The null is tested using an experiment-wide error rate of 5% with the usual normality assumption. If the null is rejected then we may conclude that the data provide sufficient evidence of an impact of the intervention - in this case, the deployment of the EDB. Failure to reject results in an inconclusive test. It should be noted, however, that the data in event time are not a true time series in the sense that the ordering of the data do not follow chronological time. As such, it is not likely that the data contain any ARIMA processes. When the data are not serially related and the hypothesized response to the intervention is a step function, the method reduces to a simple t-test of the difference between the group means.

EXHIBIT 3-1
Diagrammatic Representation of Intraday and Interday Volatility

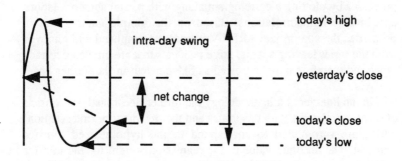

EXHIBIT 3-2
Diagrammatic Representation of the Event Time Window Used in the Test

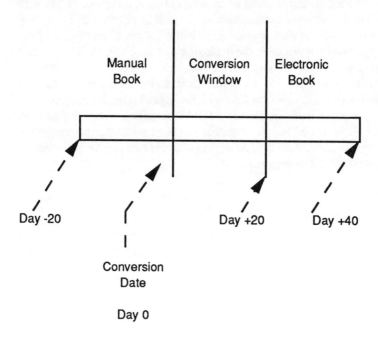

Data Analysis and Results

Excess volatility data of 685 stocks at the NYSE that were converted from the manual book to the electronic book between April 1987 and December 1989 are studied. A cross sectional analysis of price volatility data of these stocks in 'event time' during this period reveals convincing evidence that the 'excess volatility' of stocks is lower after the electronic book is installed.

This effect is detectable only when the trading volume is high and when the market for the stock is 'moving'. Additionally, the evidence does not suggest that the lower volatility has been achieved at the expense of liquidity. The observed effect may therefore be interpreted as an improvement in market quality.

Three sources of data were used in this study. These are: the implementation schedule of the Electronic Book (shown in Appendix 1) that was provided by SIAC (Securities Industry Automation Corporation); historical daily stock price and volume data purchased from CRSP (Center for Research on Securities Prices); and the Wall Street Journal Index.

The event window used is sixty trading days wide (there are approximately 22 trading days per month). This includes a 20-day 'comparison period' prior to EDB (Electronic Display Book) implementation during which the stock is assumed to be traded using the manual book. The comparison period is followed by a 20-day period, called a 'learning period' during which no data are sampled. The test period comprises the 20 days following the learning period when the stock is assumed to be completely traded on the EDB. The class variable 'Trading' is then assigned a value of 'manual' for trading days in the comparison period and a value of 'EDB' for trading days in the test period.

Ideally, we would expect there to be forty observations per stock; twenty on each side of the treatment. However, the CRSP file does not contain all the required data values for all trading days. Intraday high and low prices are available only for trading days since April of 1987. Stocks with conversion dates prior to April 1987 were also dropped from the sample. Stocks with fewer than thirty observations were eliminated to ensure that at least ten observations will be made in each side of the EDB implementation. Observations of stock prices of less

than five dollars and trading volumes of less than 10,000 shares per day
and observations made during the market breaks of 1987 and 1989 were
dropped. These elimination procedures left a sample of 795 stocks with
24,645 observations from a list of some 1,200 stocks in the
implementation schedule.

A sample cleaning procedure was used to reduce the effect of
uncontrolled external events that may change the stock volatility in the
test or comparison period. For each stock in the implementation
schedule, the WSJI (Wall Street Journal Index) was searched for unusual
events in a 4-month window surrounding the implementation date. Data
for stocks that were under the influence of external events were
considered 'noisy' and removed from the sample since an observed
difference in stock price volatility between the two periods may be due
to the external event rather than the EDB. This process resulted in the
elimination of 3876 observations (110 stocks) out of a total of 24,645
observations (795 stocks) leaving 20,769 observations (685 stocks).
The external events that caused a stock to be classified as 'noisy' were
taken from the synthesis of event studies by Copeland and Weston
(1988) and include takeovers, mergers, new listings, bond rating
changes, lawsuits, new stock offerings, and stock buybacks.

COMPUTATION OF EXCESS INTRADAY VOLATILITY

The hypothesis of this study concerns intraday volatility that is in
excess of that explained by interday volatility and is defined in terms of
a linear regression model as the residual when intraday volatility is
regressed against the interday volatility (controlling for price). This
quantity is the response variable of this quasi-experimental study and is
referred to here as "excess volatility". The regression model is described
in Chapter 3.

Exhibit 4-1 shows the results of the regression analysis. The model
explains over 42% of the sum of squared deviations from the mean
intraday volatility of all 20,769 observations. The residuals of this
model represent a portion of the intraday volatility that is not explained
by the interday volatility and therefore, after Barnea (1974), may contain
information on trading mechanisms and market microstructure. This
regression serves as a way of separating mechanism information from
economic information. The excess intraday volatility is then computed

as: y = 2.411 + r, where 2.411 is the intercept term in the regression model and r represents the residuals of the regression model.

Check for Parallelism of Control Variables

The objective of the design is to make inferences about the treatment means of the response variable y=excess volatility. The 'treatment' here is the trading method which has two levels. ('manual' or 'EDB'). The level of the trading volume, v, is also measured in each observation since it is expected that v affects price volatility (Tauchen and Pitts 1983, Ohlson and Penman 1985). By including v as a covariate in the design, variation in y that is associated with v is removed from the error sum of squares and the treatment means of the response (excess volatility) are adjusted for v before the means are compared.

The analysis hinges on the assumption that treatment effects are homogeneous over all values of v. That is to say, if y were plotted against v for the two levels of the treatment variable one would obtain two lines that are parallel to each other and separated by a distance that is equal to the treatment effect. To use this analysis, therefore, it must be determined whether this parallelism holds. A check for parallelism may be made by testing the interaction between the treatment and the covariate with the null hypothesis as Ho: No interaction exists between trading method and trading volume. The effect of the treatment is uniform over all values of trading volume.

To test this hypothesis, an interaction term is added to the regression model used in the test for trading method. The linear model used for this check is

$$y = a + b1*v + b2*M + b4*S + b5*T + b6*vT + b7*ST + b8*TM$$

The variables are:
y = Excess volatility [response variable]
v = Trading volume [covariate]
M = Market movement [control variable which indicates whether the market is 'moving', i.e., changed by 3 ticks or more that day]
S = Specialist [control variable which identifies the specialist operating the market for the stock]
T = Trading method [treatment. manual or EDB].

The interaction terms are:

vT = Trading volume times the trading method; used to determine whether the effect of the treatment is dependent on the level of the trading volume.
ST = Interaction between trading method and specialist.
TM = Interaction between trading method and the price movement in the market for the stock.

The result of this regression (Exhibit 4-2) shows that the partial sum of squares of the vT interaction yields an F-ratio of $F=64.1$ with a p-value of less than 0.001. The data provide sufficient evidence to reject the null hypothesis and to conclude that the slopes are not homogeneous. That is the effect of the treatment is not uniform over all values of trading volume v, but is different at different values of v.

A MODIFIED MODEL FOR A HETEROGENEOUS SYSTEM

The high level of interaction between the treatment and the covariate requires that the analysis be made over smaller ranges of the covariate. To do so, variable called 'Vrange' is defined and the range of trading volumes in the sample is subdivided consistent with normal perceptions of trading activity. Stocks trading more than 500,000 shares per day are considered 'active' or 'liquid' issues (Amihud and Mendelson 1989) and are given special consideration by the specialists at the NYSE. Similarly, those trading less than 100,000 shares are treated as 'inactive'. Using these perceptions as a basis we may divide the data into four ranges of trading volumes as follows:

High trading volume: More than 500,000 shares per day
Moderate trading volume: 250,000 to 500,000 shares per day
Low trading volume: 100,000 to 250,000 shares per day
Thin trading volume: Less than 100,000 shares traded.

A heterogeneous linear model that may be used to test for treatment effects within each of these range of trading volumes is stated as follows:

$$y = a + b1*v + b2*M + b3*S + b4*V + b5*VT + b6*vV + b7*vTV + b8*ST + b9*T(M\ V)$$

where the new terms introduced are:

V = 'Vrange' or range of trading volumes

vV = interaction between trading volume and Vrange

vTV = Interaction between trading volume and the treatment within each range of trading volumes

T(M V) = A nested structure used to set up interactions between the treatment T and class variables M and V so that means of the response variable may be obtained at all combinations of their levels.

In Exhibit 4-3, the F-statistic for the partial sum of squares contributed by the vTV term shows that the variation of excess volatility with trading volume for the two types of trading methods may be considered to be parallel within each range. The modified model is therefore used to test the hypothesis regarding trading methods.

TEST OF THE TRADING METHOD HYPOTHESIS

Excess volatility data are analyzed using the modified linear model that includes one covariate (Trading volume) and three control variables (Specialist, Market movement, and Vrange) in addition to the treatment (Trading method). The results of the analysis are presented in Exhibit 4-4, Exhibit 4-5, and Exhibit 4-6.

Exhibit 4-4 shows that the model being proposed explains approximately 55% of the variation in intraday volatility and 22% of the variation in the excess intraday volatility. Exhibit 4-5 shows the partial sum of squares for each of the parameters of the model for excess volatility. The partial sum of squares of a parameter is the additional sum of squared deviations accounted for by the parameter after all the other parameters and their interactions have been entered into the model.

It is evident that significant interactions exist between the class variables Vrange and Market movement with the treatment (Trading method). Were it not for this interaction, the hypothesis could be tested simply by evaluating the partial sum of squares attributable to the treatment. However, because of the interactions the effect of the treatment on excess volatility may only be assessed at specified values of these control variables. This is made possible by including the nested structure T (M V) where T is the treatment (trading method), M indicates whether the is moving, and V is one of four trading volume ranges.

We can now use the nested structure to compare the adjusted mean excess volatility between the two levels of the treatment (Trading method='EDB' or 'Manual') for all combinations of the levels of the control variables M (Market movement) and V (Vrange). A table of the characteristics of each of these treatment groups is presented in Exhibit 4-6 and the pairwise comparisons between adjusted excess volatilities are made in Exhibit 4-7. It can be seen from these comparisons that the treatment (Trading method) does affect excess volatility but that it does so only when the market for the stock in question is moving in one direction or another by 3 or more ticks per day and when the trading volume for the stock in question is more than 100,000 shares per day.

Under other conditions the test is inconclusive under normal reasoning of statistical inference testing. However, in this case, given the power of the test afforded by the large sample size the data suggest that the excess volatility under certain conditions has not changed with the implementation of the EDB. In particular under low trading volumes or when the market is 'static' (not moving), the excess volatility is about the same under either trading method.

A CHECK FOR TREND EFFECTS

Although causality may not be inferred from such a test, it is helpful to check the obvious rival hypotheses that, if true, would render the detected association between excess volatility and trading method a spurious statistic. One such rival hypothesis is that of a 'trend effect' which may be stated as follows: If an external event not in the model causes a gradual decrease in excess volatilities over the period of the test, then the event time window used will show an "effect" of decreased volatility even when there is no effect. Alternately, if an external event such as a SEC regulation or NYSE rule causes a sudden decrease in volatility and there is a sufficient number of conversions around the date of the change, the test will show an association between conversions and a decrease in volatility although no such relationship exists. Both of these external effects are shown diagrammatically in Exhibit 4-8.

An implication of the external event hypothesis is that an 'effect' of the treatment would be observed regardless of the assignment of implementation dates. In particular, if the same set of implementation dates are incorrectly assigned to the set of stocks in the sample, the external effect will be detected as if it were a treatment effect. Exhibit 4-9 shows the result of such a test. Because of the high p-values (probability of observing the sample statistic given the null hypothesis) the null hypothesis is not rejected and we conclude that the data do not provide any evidence of external effects.

TEST OF THE LIQUIDITY HYPOTHESIS

Price volatility causes increased investor perception of risk. The result is that risk-averse investors will demand higher returns and bid the price down. In this sense volatility is 'bad' especially if it is being generated by the market mechanism. A sub-optimal market design may therefore be responsible for lowering the net capital that may be invested in the macro-economy.

It has been observed by Schwert (1990) and Amihud and Mendelson (1990), however, that volatility is not necessarily bad and, in particular, that low volatility is not necessarily good if the lowering of the volatility results in a loss of liquidity. The argument is that markets exist to provide liquidity and for any given market design a measure of volatility is needed to generate the liquidity.

One measure of liquidity is the the total dollar volume of trade that can be put through the market for a percentage change in price (Amihud and Mendelson 1989, Dubofsky and Groth 1984). A modified form of this definition is used in this study. The dollar volume of trade is computed per tick (one eighth of a dollar) rather than on a percentage basis; intraday range rather than interday change is used as a measure of the price differential; and in cases where no change in price occurs, a change of one tick is used in the computation in order to avoid division by zero.

A linear model is used to assess the effect on liquidity of the parameters in the volatility study. The model,

$$\text{Liquidity} = a + b1*S + b2*M + b3*TS + b4*T(M\ V)$$

uses the parameters;

S = Specialist effect
M = Market movement ('moving' or 'static')
TS = Interaction between trading method and specialist
T (M V) = A nested structure of trading method, Market movement, and
trading volume range.

The results of the regression and the partial sum of squares for each
parameter are shown in Exhibit 4-10. Exhibit 4-11 contains the
pairwise comparison of liquidity means. To determine whether the
implementation of the Electronic Display Book has been associated
with a change in liquidity, we test the null hypothesis that the
treatment has no association with liquidity as Ho: The liquidity of the
EDB market is is the same as that of the manual market against Ha:
The liquidity of the EDB market is different from that of the manual
market

The test of this hypothesis is carried out in Exhibit 4-11 for each
combination of levels of the control variables. These tests do not
indicate any evidence that the observed decrease in volatility is
associated with the EDB has been at the expense of lower liquidity. In
fact, the data suggests that in the range of trading volumes of 500,000
shares per day or more, the liquidity is higher when the electronic book
is used. We may therefore conclude that the quality of the EDB market
is better than the manual book market. The difference is only detectable
at high trading volumes and may not exist at low trading volumes.

INTERVENTION ANALYSIS OF THE EVENT-TIME SERIES

The analysis and interpretation of "quasi-experimental" field data over
time has been treated by Cook and Campbell (1979) and Box and Tiao
(1976). The generalized problem is that of an innovation in time in
which an 'interruption' or an 'intervention' occurs. A time series of the
response variable is available before and after the intervention. The
authors offer a methodology for the treatment of such an interrupted
time series data set.

This methodology may be used to analyze the excess volatility data
by treating them as a time series of forty observations interrupted by
the Electronic Display Book. The "treatment" is called an "intervention"
by Box and Tiao (1976) and an "interruption" by Cook and Campbell
(1979). It is noted, however, that the series of aggregate volatility data

are not a time series in the strict sense since they are not observed over chronological time but over 'event time'. For example, the third observation in the series may include data from May 4, 1987 for IBM and September 7, 1988 for Xerox. What places the third observation after the second and before the fourth is not time but the distance in time from the implementation of the electronic trading system. A second departure of this system from that treated by Cook and Campbell (1979) is that the first twenty days of data following the deployment of the EDB are removed from the series to allow time for the specialist to become used to the new technology. The two truncated ends of the series are then joined together.

The series of aggregate excess volatility data in event time are shown in Exhibits 4-12, 4-13, and 4-14 according to trading volume ranges. The data represent the aggregate excess intraday volatility adjusted for trading volume for each trading day. Time is measured as the number of trading days before the implementation of the EDB or the number of days after the 20-day training period. The adjustment for trading volume was performed by using a simple linear regression of excess volatility against volume and computing the residuals.

The hypothesis of this study is interpreted as a step change in excess volatility. Using a step transfer function to represent the intervention, a significant effect of EDB implementation is found in both the high volume and moderate volume cases. No effect of the the intervention is detected in the low volume series. These findings are consistent with a visual examination of the plots in Exhibits 4-12, 4-13, and 4-14.

Time series analysis of the data do not reveal any moving average or autoregressive properties; i.e., the data are indistinguishable from white noise and may treated as independent. The correlogram in Exhibit 4-15 plots the correlation coefficient against the lag. The dotted lines enclose a 95% confidence interval around a zero correlation. The entire correlogram lies within these limits. This indicates a lack of evidence of serial correlation; or, in other words, the data are not distinguishable from white noise.

In such cases intervention analysis of a step function reduces to a simple t-test of the difference between the means before and after the intervention. The results of the t-tests, shown in Exhibit 4-16, are consistent with the results obtained with the linear model.

EXHIBIT 4-1
Computation of Excess Volatility Linear Model

Intra = Constant + A*Inter + B*Price + C*Inter*Price + Unexplained
Where
Intra = Intraday price volatility defined as the intraday range
Inter = Interday price volatility defined as close to close
Price = Average intraday price defined as (high+low)/2

Results of the Regression

Number of observations: 20938

Parameter	Estimate	Partial SS	F	p>F
Constant	2.411			
Inter	.026768	6378	46.3	<.001
Price	.011921	71901	5225	<.001
Inter*Price	.00022787	6802	494.3	<.001

Total sum of squares for Intra   497788
Sum of squares explained by the model 209726
R-squared = 0.4213

EXHIBIT 4-2
Check for Parallelism

Source	df	SS	Mean Square	F-Ratio
Model	99	59043	596.4	54.2
Error	20669	227499	11.00	
Total	20768	286541		
R-squared		0.206		

Parameters of the Model

Source	df	partial SS	F-Ratio	p-value
Volume	1	11755	1068	<.001
Specialist	47	3195	6.18	<.001
Movement	1	29182	2651	<.001
TS	47	1129	2.18	<.001
vT	1	705.2	64.1	<.001
TM	1	85.9	7.80	0.0052

'Market movement' is an indicator variable that indicates whether the stock had moved more than 2 ticks (3 or more ticks) that trading day. 'TS' is the interaction between the treatment (trading method) and the specialist. vT is the interaction between Trading volume and Trading method. TM is the interaction between Trading method and Market movement.

EXHIBIT 4-3
Test for Parallelism with Vrange

Source	df	SS	F-Ratio	p-Value
Vrange	3	969.8	29.9	<.0001
Volume*Vrange	3	1084	33.4	<.0001
Volume*Trading*Vrange	4	61.3	1.42	0.2247

Vrange = Range of trading volumes
High trading volume: More than 500,000 shares per day
Moderate trading volume: 250,000 to 500,000 shares per day
Low trading volume: 100,000 to 250,000 shares per day
Thin trading volume: Less than 100,000 shares traded.

Volume*Vrange
Interaction between Trading volume and Vrange exists. The effect of Trading volume depends on which Vrange we are in.

Volume*Trading*Vrange
No evidence of interaction between Trading volume and method of trading (EDB versus manual) within each Vrange (range of Trading volumes).

EXHIBIT 4-4
ANOVA Table for the Linear Model

ANOVA Table for Excess Volatility

Source	df	Sum of Squares		Mean Square	F Ratio
Model	117	63461	542.4		50.2
Error	20651	223080	10.80		
Total	20768	286542			

R-Squared   0.2215

ANOVA Table for Intraday Volatility (Overall Model)

Source	df	Sum of Squares		Mean Square	F Ratio
Model	120	273187	2277		190
Error	20648	224601	10.88		
Total	20768	497788			

R-Squared   0.549

The 'Overall Model' includes the first stage regression of intraday volatility against interday volatility and price. The overall r-squared shows that more than 55% of the sum of squared deviations of intraday volatility from the mean intraday volatility of 5.539 is explained in terms of the models being proposed.

EXHIBIT 4-5
Partial Sum of Squares of Model Parameters

Dependent Variable: Excess Volatility

Parameter	df	Partial SS	Ft*	p(F>Ft)**
Volume	1	1705.8	158	<.001
Specialist	47	2888	5.69	<.001
Movement	1	21419	1983	<.001
Vrange	3	969.8	29.9	<.001
VR	3	1084	33.4	<.001
TS	47	1151	2.27	<.001
T (M V)	10	2049	19.0	<.001

* Based on error sum of squares = 223080 and error degrees of freedom = 20651 per Exhibit 4-4. Mean square error = 10.8.
** given the null hypothesis that the excess volatility is not related to the parameter in question.

Market movement = The market for the stock is considered 'moving' if the interday movement in price is 3 ticks or more; else it is considered static.

Vrange = Four different ranges of trading volumes within which the effect of trading volume is homogeneous with respect to trading method.

VR = The interaction between Vrange and Trading volume. Small p-value indicates evidence that the effect of trading volume is not homogeneous among the trading volume ranges.

TS = The interaction between trading method and specialist.

T(M V) = A nested structure for a design in which there are independent samples of T (trading method) within each combination of M (Market movement) and V (range of trading volume). This structure is helpful in setting up pairwise comparisons at each level of the control variables and is necessary because direct comparison of the sample means for trading=EDB versus trading=manual is not possible due to interaction between the control variables and the treatment.

EXHIBIT 4-6
Characteristics of Each Treatment Group

Vrange	N		Mean Trading Volume		Unadjusted Sample Means	
	Manual	EDB	Manual	EDB	Manual	EDB
Market is moving						
>500	495	502	901	915	7.69	5.50
250-500	692	635	354	354	5.42	4.33
100-250	1147	1051	162	160	4.55	4.02
<100	2113	1928	48	49	3.19	2.96
Market is static						
>500	242	254	879	857	2.71	2.09
250-500	499	449	350	348	2.05	1.96
100-250	1198	1197	156	155	1.73	1.50
<100	4186	4181	41	41	1.07	0.88

Trading volume figures are in thousands of shares per day.

EXHIBIT 4-7
Pairwise Comparison of Least Square Means

Vrange   Least Square Mean Excess Volatility

	Manual/EDB	Diff	s	t	p(t>test)
Market is moving					
>500	6.181 /4.547	1.634	2091	7.82	<.001**
250-500	4.610 /3.590	1.020	.1814	5.62	<.001**
100-250	4.438 /4.022	0.416	.1409	2.95	.0032**
<100	4.513 /4.482	0.031	.1039	0.30	.7642
Market is static					
>500	1.279 /1.143	0.136	.2965	0.46	.6456
250-500	1.316 /1.238	0.078	.2147	0.36	.7188
100-250	1.745 /1.570	0.175	.1349	1.30	.1936
<100	2.554 /2.516	0.038	.0722	0.53	.5962

Basis: Mean Square Error = 10.8, s = sqrt[(RMS/n1) + (RMS/n2)]
   n1 = sample size for manual trading
   n2 = sample size for EDB trading

The experiment-wide error rate is held at a=0.05. There are eight pairwise comparisons made. Thus the pairwise error rate is ap=0.05/8 = 0.0063. When the p-value for any comparison is less than 0.0063, we reject the null hypothesis for that pair. Such rejections are noted with a double asterisk (**).

EXHIBIT 4-8

Types of External Effects

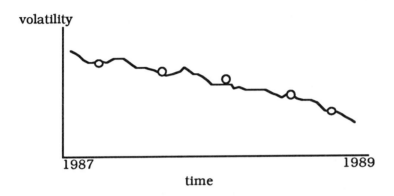

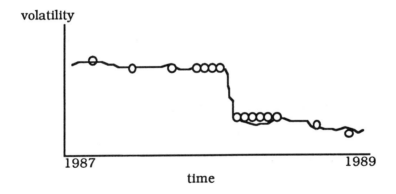

EXHIBIT 4-9
Hypothesis Test Using Incorrect Assignment of Implementation Dates
Pairwise Comparison of Least Square Means

Vrange   Least Square Mean Excess Volatility

	Manual	EDB	Diff	two-tail p-Value
Market is moving				
>500	4.34	4.24	0.10	0.7278
250-500	4.38	3.75	0.63	0.0870
100-250	3.81	3.78	0.02	0.8658
<100	4.57	4.46	0.11	0.7256
Market is static				
>500	2.51	2.72	0.20	0.5099
250-500	2.64	2.06	0.58	0.1101
100-250	2.20	1.95	0.25	0.0535
<100	3.10	3.14	0.04	0.8991

Basis: Mean Square Error = 8.996, s = sqrt[(RMS/n1) + (RMS/n2)]
        n1 = sample size for manual trading
        n2 = sample size for EDB trading

The 'p-Value' is the probability of the observation given the null
hypothesis. The experiment-wide error rate is held at a=0.05. There are
eight pairwise comparisons made. Thus the pairwise error rate is
ap=0.05/8 = 0.0063. When the p-value for any comparison is less than
0.0063, we reject the null hypothesis for that pair and conclude that the
data are sufficient evidence that a difference in excess volatility exists
between manual and electronic trading. Such rejections are noted with a
double asterisk (**).

EXHIBIT 4-10
ANOVA Table for Liquidity

Source	df	Sum of Squares	Mean Square	F
Model	125	2219006	17752	103
Error	20812	3594156	172.70	
Total	20937	5813162		

R-Squared   0.3800

Partial sum of squares attributable to each model parameter
Liquidity = f(S,M,T,B,V)

Parameter	df	Partial SS	F	p-Value
Specialist (S)	47	31730	3.91	<.001
Movement (M)	1	6630.4	38.4	<.001
Trading*Specialist	47	14792	1.82	.0006
T (V M)	25	1995533	462	<.001

The 'p-Value' refers to the probability of making these sample observations if the null hypothesis were true. The null hypothesis for each parameter states that liquidity is not affected by the parameter or that there is not relationship between liquidity and the parameter in question.

Liquidity is here defined as 0.001*price*volume divided by the intraday volatility. The factor of 0.001 is used to avoid large numbers. The equation may be paraphrased as the dollar volume of trades that can be put through for a unit tick swing in intraday prices.

'Market movement' is a class variable with two levels that indicates whether the price has moved by 3 or more ticks during the trading day. 'Trading' is the treatment and is either 'manual' or 'EDB'. The structure 'T (V M)' is used to assess the effect of Trading (T) at all combinations of Trading volume range (V) and Market movement (M).

EXHIBIT 4-11

Comparison of Liquidity Means

Vrange   Adjusted Mean Liquidity

	Manual	EDB	Change	s	p (two-tail)
Market is moving.					
>500	31.185	36.331	5.146	.8368	<.001**
250-500	14.024	16.094	2.070	.5641	.0022**
100-250	6.758	7.178	0.420	1.186	.7188
<100	2.129	2.313	0.184	.540	.7338
Market is static					
>500	48.297	52.638	4.341	.7259	<.001**
250-500	20.856	21.466	0.610	.4161	.1416
100-250	9.816	9.932	0.116	.8593	.8920
<100	2.845	2.942	0.097	.2883	.7338

Basis: Mean Square Error = 174.5, $s = sqrt[(RMS/n1) + (RMS/n2)]$
        $n1$ = sample size for manual trading
        $n2$ = sample size for EDB trading

The 'p-Value' is the probability of the observation given the null hypothesis. The experiment-wide error rate is held at $a=0.05$. There are eight pairwise comparisons made. Thus the pairwise error rate is $ap=0.05/8 = 0.0063$. When the p-value for any comparison is less than 0.0063, we reject the null hypothesis for that pair and conclude that the data are sufficient evidence that a difference in liquidity exists between manual and electronic trading. Such rejections are noted with a double asterisk (**).

EXHIBIT 4-12

Daily Aggregate Adjusted Excess Volatility in Event Time

High Trading Volume

Mean Excess Volatility Adjusted for Trading Volume: Market is moving, Trading volume is high (more than 500,000 shares per day)

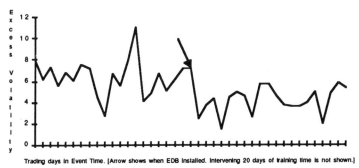

Trading days in Event Time. [Arrow shows when EDB installed. Intervening 20 days of training time is not shown.]

EXHIBIT 4-13
Daily Aggregate Adjusted Excess Volatility in Event Time
Moderate Trading Volume

Mean Excess Volatility Adjusted for Trading Volume: Market is moving, Trading volume is moderate (250,000 to 500,000 shares per day)

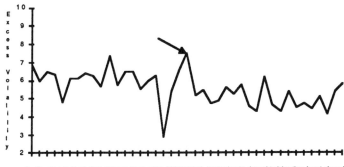

Trading days in Event Time. [Arrow shows when EDB installed. Intervening 20 days of training time is not shown.]

EXHIBIT 4-14
Daily Aggregate Adjusted Excess Volatility in Event Time
Low Trading Volume

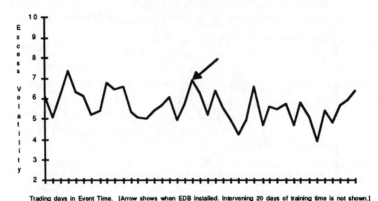

Mean Excess Volatility Adjusted for Trading Volume: Market is moving, Trading volume is low (100,000 to 250,000 shares per day)

Trading days in Event Time. [Arrow shows when EDB installed. Intervening 20 days of training time is not shown.]

EXHIBIT 4-15
Correlogram
Test for White Noise of Event-Time Series

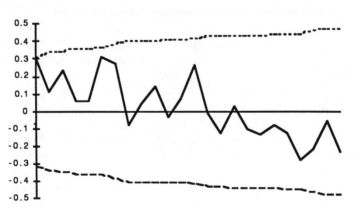

EXHIBIT 4-16
T-test: Unequal Variance
Test of the Excess Volatility Hypothesis

Vrange   Mean Adjusted Excess Volatility

	Manual μ/s	EDB μ/s	t	DF	p-Value
Market is Moving					
>500	6.35/9.03	4.11/5.53	4.72	816	<.001**
250-500	6.07/5.37	4.98/4.01	4.21	1274	<.001**
100-250	5.90/4.19	5.37/3.96	3.00	2194	.0027**
<100	4.95/3.94	4.71/3.83	1.92	4023	.0546
Market is Static					
>500	1.45/3.81	0.91/3.82	1.57	493	.1170
250-500	2.71/2.44	2.63/2.43	0.54	937	.5864
100-250	3.10/2.24	2.87/2.08	2.52	2381	.0119
<100	2.86/1.75	2.67/1.55	5.33	8252	<.001**

1. The excess volatility is adjusted for variation with volume.
2. The p-value is the probability of obtaining the sample t-value given the null hypothesis that no difference exists between the manually traded and electronically traded excess volatilities.
3. Because of the observed differences between manual and EDB sample variances, the p-values are checked without the equal variance assumption.
4. The apparently 'significant' result at <100 thousand shares traded per day in a static market is ascribed to the large sample size and high power of the test. The actual difference in volatility is 0.19.
5. 'Vrange' is the the range of trading volumes stated in thousands of shares traded per day.
6. The experiment-wide error rate is held at a=0.05. There are eight pairwise comparisons made. Thus the pairwise error rate is ap=0.05/8 = 0.0063. When the p-value for any comparison is less than 0.0063, we reject the null hypothesis for that pair. Such rejections are noted with a double asterisk (**).

Summary and Conclusions

The 'case study' method of business research espoused by Lucas (1974), Markus (1983), Allen (1988), and Benbasat (1987), is used in this study to overcome problems in assessing the impact of information systems. First a theory of the impact of information systems is formulated. Then unambiguous and testable implications of the theory are deduced for a specific IT implementation. Then if 'fortuitous' conditions allow, these implications are tested in a field setting using quasi-experimental methods (Cook and Campbell 1979).

The field setting enhances realism and generalizability of results when compared with controlled laboratory experiments. The targeting of specific systems overcomes the problems related to the identification of the appropriate response variable. This study has targeted exchange automation systems and uses tests on a specific implementation of electronic trading in the NYSE to test the implications of the theory that market automation changes the price discovery process and therefore the price behavior.

Extant economic theories of markets and market microstructure may be used to formulate a theory of of the price effects of exchange automation. Studies by financial economists such as Barnea (1974), Beja (1979), Amihud and Mendelson (1989) and others indicate that trading mechanisms affect price behavior especially with regard to short term components of price volatility. Further, theories of market automation proposed by Garbade and Silber (1979), Amihud and Mendelson (1990), Schwartz (1985), Miller (1989) and others all indicate that exchange automation changes the microstructure of the market. Based on these studies we deduce and test the theory that automation changes the component of price volatility that is generated by the trading mechanism.

To test this theory we study the implementation of the Electronic Display Book on the floor of the New York Stock Exchange and postulate that the excess intraday price volatility that may be ascribed to trading mechanism will change when the EDB is deployed.

Fortuitously, the EDB was deployed over a three year period using over 100 implementation dates to convert about a thousand stocks to the new technology. This allows the use of 'event time' methodologies to cancel out concomitant historical effects from the quasi-experimental design. Further, economic effects are factored out of intraday changes by using a regression technique which leaves residuals, termed 'excess intraday volatility'. This quantity is ascribed to trading mechanism effects and is therefore postulated as the appropriate response variable for measuring the impact of the information system.

Using trading volume and market movement as control variables, it is found that at trading volumes higher than 100,000 shares per day and in cases where the daily price movement is at least three ticks, the excess intraday price volatility of stocks is lower after EDB implementation. At lower trading volumes or when the price is not moving (by three ticks or more), no difference in excess volatility is detected.

Volatility is an important property of markets. In particular, lower volatility is a desirable property in market design. This is because in a mean-variance world of risk averse utility maximizers governed by the efficient market hypothesis (Markowitz 1959, Sharpe 1963, Fama 1970) investors will demand additional returns to bear the excess volatility generated by the market mechanism. As a result the overall investment into productive assets in the macro economy would be less than it would have been had the stock market been frictionless.

However, Amihud and Mendelson (1989) have argued (see Exhibit 2-1) that the only real function of markets is to provide liquidity and that liquidity and volatility are related. Market design that lowers volatility is desirable only to the extent that this does not adversely affect liquidity. A test on liquidity is therefore performed and it is found that there is no evidence that at least one measure of liquidity is lower after the deployment of the electronic limit order book.

We may therefore conclude as follows: The implementation of the electronic trading system has had a measurable impact on price behavior. Volatility has been lowered without also decreasing liquidity. The 'quality' of the EDB market is therefore considered to be higher than that of the manual limit order book market.

Since Garbade and Silber's (1978) paper on the impact of new technology on the narrowing of bid-ask spreads there have been little empirical evidence of the effect of automation in securities markets although the last decade has seen the greatest push toward automation of trading in history. This paper breaks significant new ground in this line of inquiry. It shows that the impact of technology can be measured and that such a measurement shows that the automation of the limit order book within the specialist system at the NYSE has served to decrease the frictional losses due to market mechanism. Technical innovations in securities trading may not be evaluated en masse but must be studied within their own context. For example, uncontrolled 'screen trading' may produce highly volatile and erratic price discovery processes as speculated by Brady (1988) and others but such was not found to be the case when the specialist is assisted rather than displaced by the computer. The evidence also suggests that automation changes the microstructure of the market and may therefore not be ignored when studying the effect of trading mechanisms.

The methodology used in this paper may be used to test any changes in market microstructure as well as the introduction of automatic trading systems. The failure of the "big bang" screen trading system in London (Clemons and Weber 1990) and the inability of the INTEX computerized commodity futures trading market to gain market share (Figlewski 1986) have raised new questions and concerns about computerized trading. The vision of the completely automated 24-hour market first described in the '70s by proponents of the ITS (Intermarket Trading System) (Black 1977) and later refined by Amihud and Mendelson (1985) as the ICTS (Integrated Computerized Trading System) may be tested using the methodology of this work prior to wholesale introduction as was done in London.

We suggest here that the impact of information systems as a whole may be best understood not in one large cross sectional study but by an orderly accumulation of knowledge through many small and highly directed research where the system and the application are well defined and well understood by the researcher. The expansion of these findings to other automated trading systems and other markets may be performed using the dependent variables and methodologies suggested by this paper. The Tokyo and Toronto Stock Exchanges are partially automated. Some stocks are computerized while others continue to trade manually. Tokyo data may be difficult to obtain but Toronto data are available directly from the exchange.

Both the SEC and the NYSE have promoted techniques to artificially control volatility that they ascribe to program traders. The techniques used are called "circuit breakers". The data tapes maintained by the SIAC contain records of each invocation of the "sidecar" circuit breaker. Intraday price data may be used to determine whether these interventions by the sidecar benefit the market or whether, as many

suspect, the artificial reduction in price volatility is at the expense of
liquidity and a poor market quality.

The evaluation of specialist performance has been the subject of
many studies notable those of Barnea (1974), Beja (1977), and Beja and
Hakanson (1987). The empirical tests have been inconclusive. Only a
minor modification of the present study is necessary to test specialist
performance using the 'excess intraday volatility' as a dependent
variable. The model may then be used to test simulated markets using
an expert system to replace the specialist (Hakanson, Beja, and Kale
1985). The important distinction between an expert system market and
the specialist market is that the expert system does not take a position
in the market and carries no inventory. In this regard it is similar to the
'saitori' in the Tokyo Stock Exchange. The saitori acts as a clerk and
manages the limit order book but is forbidden from trading on his own
account.

Automated secondary exchanges such as Cincinnati and Boston
provide additional opportunities to study market automation.
Cincinnati, for example, uses a highly computerized version of 'screen
trading'. Those stocks listed on the NYSE but also traded on the
secondary exchanges via the ITS (Intermarket Trading System) may be
compared to non-ITS stocks to determine whether the computerized
secondary markets are able to offer better liquidity via screen trading. (I
am indebted to Professor Yakov Amihud for this suggestion.)

Much has been made of the 'floorless' and computerized trading at
the London exchange; yet the market performed poorly during a 1989
break and the exchange has since lost market share to European
exchanges and to the large brokerage houses. London's version of
computerization may provide an important example of automation gone
wrong. A scientific case study of excess volatilities may uncover
reasons for its failure and lead to better market design in the future.

The introduction of the 'Globex' screen trading and trade
information system at the CBOT (Chicago Board of Trade) and other
innovations in pit trading such as hand held terminals are important
developments in the commodities and options markets and their impact
on market properties may be evaluated using a similar study. Early
evaluations of new systems provide not only a deeper understanding of
markets and the automation technologies but offer feedback to market
designers. Research into market microstructure and exchange
automation is gaining new importance with increasing emphasis on

computerization. Studies such as this work serve to increase the chances that new market designs and the use of automation in trading systems are appropriate and optimal.

Bibliography

Ackoff, Russell L., *Management Misinformation Systems*, Management Science, Vol. 14 No. 4 Dec (1967) pp. B147-B156

Allen, Anne E. and Lois Zarembo, *The Display Book: The NYSE Specialists' Electronic Workstation*, in Lucas and Schwartz (1989) pp. 205-213

Amihud, Yakov, Thomas Ho, and Robert Schwartz, *Market Making and the Changing Structure of the Securities Industry*, Lexington Books, Lexington, MA, (1985), 311 pages

Amihud, Yakov, Thomas Ho, and Robert Schwartz, *Overview of the Changing Securities Markets*, in Amihud, Ho, and Schwartz (1985) pp. 1-15

Amihud, Yakov and Haim Mendelson, *An Integrated Computerized Trading System*, in Amihud, Ho, and Schwartz (1985) pp. 217-235

Amihud, Yakov, and Haim Mendelson, *Asset Pricing and the Bid-Ask Spread*, Journal of Financial Economics, Vol. 17 No. 2, Dec (1986) pp. 223-249

Amihud, Yakov and Haim Mendelson, *Trading Mechanisms and Stock Returns: An Empirical Investigation*, The Journal of Finance, 42 No. 3, July (1987)

Amihud, Yakov and Haim Mendelson, *Liquidity, Volatility, and Exchange Automation*, Journal of Accounting, Auditing, and Finance Vol. 3 No. 4 Fall (1988) pp. 369-395

Amihud, Yakov and Haim Mendelson, *The Effects of Computer Based Trading On Volatility and Liquidity*, in Lucas and Schwartz (1989) pp. 59-85

Amihud, Yakov and Haim Mendelson, *Market Microstructure and Price Discovery on the Tokyo Stock Exchange*, Japan and the World Economy, Vol. 1 (1989) pp. 341-370

Amihud, Yakov and Haim Mendelson, *Explaining intraday and overnight price behavior: Comment*, The Journal of Portfolio Management, Winter (1989), pp. 85-86

Amihud, Yakov and Haim Mendelson, *Options Markets Integration: An Evaluation*, Unpublished Manuscript, Chicago Board of Options Exchange, January, (1990) 89 pages

Amihud, Yakov, Haim Mendelson, and Maurizio Murgia, *Stock Market Microstructure and Return Volatility: Evidence from Italy*, Journal of Banking and Finance, v.14 (1990), pp. 423-440

Anthony, R.N., *A Framework for the Analysis of Planning and Control Systems*, Harvard Graduate School of Business Administration, (1965)

Bagehot, W., *The Only Game in Town*, Financial Analysts Journal, v. 27, March-April (1971) pp. 12-14

Bailey, James E. and Sammy W. Pearson, *Development of a Tool for Measuring and Analyzing Computer User Satisfaction*, Management Science, Vol. 29 (1983) pp. 530-544

Ball, Andrew, *What Do We Know About Market Efficiency*, Working Paper, University of Iowa, (1990), 37 pages.

Bayley, Molly G., *Technology Meets Regulation*, in Saunders and White (1986) pp. 63-71

Bakos, Y. J., *Dependent Variables for the Study of Firm and Industry Level Impacts of Information Technology*, Proceedings of the Eighth International Conference on Information Systems, (1987) pp.10-23

Barnea, Amir, *Performance Evaluation of NYSE Specialists*, Journal of Financial and Quantitative Analysis, Vol. 9 September (1974) pp. 511-535

Baumol, William J., *The Stock Market and Economic Efficiency*, Fordham University Press, NY, (1965), 95 pages

Beitman, W., *Artificial Intelligence Applications in Business*, Ablex Press, Norwood, NJ, (1984)

Beja, Avraham, and Nils Hakansson, *Dynamic Market Processes and the Rewards of Up-to-Date Information*, The Journal of Finance, Vol. 32 May (1977) pp. 291-304

Benbasat, I., D. Goldstein, and M. Mead, *The Case Research Strategy in Studies of Information System"*, MIS Quarterly, Vol. 11 No. 3, (1987) pp. 369-388

Bender, D., *Financial Impact of Information Processing*, Journal of MIS, Vol. 3, Summer (1986), pp. 232-238

Berman, Marc L., Technology and the Clearing Function", in Saunders and White (1986), pp. 167-169

The Securities Markets, Twentieth Century Fund, Inc., NY, (1935), 865 pages.

Black, Fischer, *Toward a Fully Automated Stock Exchange*, Financial Analysts Journal, July-August, (1971), pp. 29-35,44

Black, Fischer, *A Fully Automated Stock Exchange*, Financial Analysts Journal, November-December, (1971), pp. 24-28,86-87

Black, Fischer, *Does Technology Matter?*, in Lucas and Schwartz (1989), pp. 151-152.

Blume, M.E., Craig Mackinlay, and Bruce Terker, *Order Imbalances and Stock Price Movements on October 19 and 20, 1987*, The Journal of Finance, Vol. 44 No. 4 Sep (1989)

Box, G.E.P. and G.C. Tiao, *Intervention Analysis With Applications to Economic and Environmental Problems*, Journal of the American Statistical Association, Vol. 70, (1976) pp. 70-79

Boyles, Gerald V. and Darcy R. Carr, *Black Monday 1987 Revisited*, Business & Economics Review, Vol. 35 No. 2, Spring (1989)

Brady, Nicholas F., *Report of the Presidential Task Force on Market Mechanisms*, U.S. Government Printing Office, Washington, DC, (1988)

Branch, Ben and David P. Echevarria, *The Impact of Bid-Ask Prices on Market Anomalies*, The Financial Review, May 1991, pp. 249-268

Braun, Helmut and John S. Chandler, *Predicting Stock Market Behavior Through Rule Induction: An Application of the Learning From Example Approach*, in Trippi and Turban (1990), pp. 78-93

Breese, Jack, *An Expert System for Decision Analysis in Securities Trading*, in Trippi and Turban (1990), pp. 53-61

Breese, Jack S., *Securities Trading and Arbitrage*, in Proceedings of the First Annual Conference on Expert Systems in Business and Finance, IEEE, (1987)

Bresnahan, Timothy F., *Measuring the Spillovers from Technical Advance: Mainframe Computers in Financial Service*, American Economic Review, Vol. 76 No. 4, Sep. (1986) pp. 742-755

Brennan, M. J., and E.S. Schwartz, *Arbitrage in Stock Index Futures*, The Journal of Business Vol. 63 No. pt. 2, (1990) pp. S7-S31

Brown, Jim, *New Trading Net in Place at Boston Stock Exchange*, Network World, Vol. 5 No. 45, Nov. 7, (1988), pp. 2-6

Brown, Keith C., W.V. Harlow, and Seha M. Tinic, *How Rational Investors Deal With Uncertainty*, Journal of Applied Corporate Finance, Fall, (1989), pp. 45-58

Brown, S.J., and J.B Warner, *Measuring Security Price Performance*, Journal of Financial Economics, Sep (1980) pp. 205-258

Brown, S.J., and J.B. Warner, *Using Daily Stock Returns: the Case of Event Studies*, The Journal of Financial Economics, March (1985), pp. 3-31

Burrell, G. and G. Morgan, *Sociological Paradigms and Organizational Analysis*, Heinemann Publishing, London, (1979)

Buser, Stephen A. and K.C. Chan, *NASDAQ National Market System Offerings and the Ohio Blue Sky Law*, The National Association of Securities Dealers, (1986)

Clemons, E. K., *A DSS Architecture for Subjective, Loosely Constrained, Data Intensive Problem Domain*, in Proceedings of the Hawaii International Conference on System Sciences, IEEE (1987) pp. 707-714

Clemons, Eric K. and Bruce W. Weber, *Making the Technology Investment Decision: Barclays De Zoete Wedd's TRADE System*, Working paper number 89-03-08, Department of Decision Sciences, The Wharton School, University of Pennsylvania, March, (1989), 28 pages.

Clemons, Eric K. and Bruce W. Weber, *Turmoil, Transparency, and Tea: The Impact of Information Technology on the London Stock Exchange*, Working paper 89-06-03, Department of Decision Sciences, The Wharton School, University of Pennsylvania, February, (1990), 25 pages.

Clemons, E. K., and Jennifer T. Adams, *Global Competition in Corporate Capital Markets*, in Lucas and Schwartz (1989) pp. 286-304

Cohen, Kalman J., Robert M. Conroy, and Steven F. Maier, *Order Flow and Quality of the Market*, in Amihud, Ho, and Schwartz (1985) pp. 93-112

Cohen, Kalman, and Robert Schwartz, *An Electronic Call Market: Its Design and Desirability*, in Lucas and Schwartz (1989) pp. 15-58

Cook, Thomas D. and Donald T. Campbell, *Quasi Experimentation: Design and Analysis Issues for Field Settings*, Rand McNally College Publishing Company, Chicago 1979, pp. 207-293

Cooper, Kerry, John C. Groth, and William E. Avera, *Liquidity, Exchange Listing, and Common Stock Performance*, Working Paper, Texas A&M, College of Business, Dept. of Finance, Aug. (1983)

Cooper, Randolph H. and Robert H. Zmud, *Information Technology Implementation Research: A Technological Diffusion Approach*, Management Science, Vol. 36 No. 2 (1990) pp. 123-139

Copeland, Thomas E. and J. Fred Weston, *Financial Theory and Corporate Policy*, Addison-Wesley Publishing Company, Reading, MA, (1988) pp. 361-400

Cox, Charles C. and Bruce A. Kohn, *Regulatory Implications of Computerized Communications in Securities Markets*, in Saunders and White (1986), pp. 7-18

Cron, W.L. and M.G. Sobol, *The Relationship Between Computerization and Performance: A Strategy for Maximizing the Economic Benefits of Computerization*, Information and Management, v. 6, (1983), pp. 171-181

Crowston, Kevin and Michael Treacy, *Assessing the Impact of Information Technology on Enterprise Level Performance*, Proceedings of the Seventh International Conference on Information Systems, (1986) pp. 299-310

Davis, Jeffry L., *The Intermarket Trading System and the Cincinnati Experiment*, in Amihud, Ho, and Schwartz (1985) pp. 269-283

Demsetz, H., *The Cost of Transacting*, The Quarterly Journal of Economics, v. 82, (1968), pp. 33-53

Dodd, P., and J. Warner, *On Corporate Governance: A Study of Proxy Contests*, Journal of Financial Economics, v. 11, (1983) pp. 401-438

Doll, William J. and Gholamreza Torkzadeh, *The Measure of End-User Computing Satisfaction*, MIS Quarterly, Vol. 12 (1988) pp. 259-273

Dubofsky, David A. and John C. Groth, *Exchange Listing and Stock Liquidity*, The Journal of Financial Research, Vol. 7 No. 4 Winter (1984)

Dudda, Soumitra, and Shashi Shekhar, *Bond Rating: A Non-Conservative Application of Neural Networks*, in Trippi and Turban (1990), pp. 271-282

Edgeworth, F.Y., *Mathematical Psychics*, (1881), in London School of Economics, "Papers Relating to Political Economy", Macmillan and Company, London, 1926

Edwards, Franklin R., *Technology and the New Regulatory Challenge in Futures Markets*, in Saunders and White (1986), pp. 171-179

Edwards, Franklin R., *Does Futures Trading Increase Stock Market Volatility?*, Financial Analysts Journal, Vol. 44 No. 1, Jan (1988) pp. 63-69

Edwards, Franklin R., *The Crash: A Report on the Reports*, in Lucas and Schwartz (1989), pp. 86-111

Ewing, Tom, *NASDAQ System Revolutionizes Trading*, Information Week, Oct. 27, (1986)

Falk, Peter S., *Upstairs Trading*, in Amihud, Ho, and Schwartz (1985) pp. 151-153

Fama, Eugene, *The Behavior of Stock Market Prices*, Journal of Business, Vol. 38, (1965) pp. 34-105

Fama, Eugene, *Perspectives on October 1987: What Did We Learn From the Crash?*, Working Paper No. 232, Center for Research on Security Prices, University of Chicago, April (1988) 14 pages.

Feltham, Gerald A., *The Value of Information*, The Accounting Review, Oct., (1968) pp. 684-696

Figlewski, Stephen, *Options Arbitrage in Imperfect Markets*, The Journal of Finance, Vol. 44 No. 6, Dec (1989) pp. 1289-1311

Finnerty, J. E. and H. Y. Park, *Empirical Evidence on Stock Index Arbitrage: the Case of Program Trading*, BEBR Faculty Working paper, University of Illinois, Urbana (1987)

Finnerty, J. E. and H. Y. Park, *Stock Index Futures: Does the Tail Wag the Dog?*, Financial Analysts Journal, Vol. 43 No. 2, Mar (1987) pp. 57-61

Floyd, Stephen W. and Bill Wooldridge, *Path Analysis of the Relationship between Competitive Strategy, Information Technology, and Financial Performance*, Journal of Management Information Systems, v. 7, Summer (1990), pp. 47-64

Freund, William C., *A New World and the New York Stock Exchange*, Journal of Accounting, Auditing, and Finance, Vol. 1 No. 1, Winter (1986)

Furbush, Dean, *Program Trading and Price Movement:
Evidence From the October 1987 Market Crash*,
Financial Management, Autumn (1988) pp. 68-83

Gallagher, Charles A., *Perceptions of the Value of a
Management Information System*, Academy of
Management Journal, Vol. 17 No. 1, Mar (1974) pp.
46-55

Galliers, Robert D., *In Search of a Paradigm for
Information Systems Research*, in Mumford (1985)
pp. 281-297

Garbade, Kenneth D. and William L. Silber, *Technology,
Communication, and the Performance of Financial
Markets*, The Journal of Finance, Vol. 33 No. 3,
June, (1978), pp. 819-832

Garbade, Kenneth D. and William L Silber, *Structural
Organization of Secondary Markets: Clearing
Frequency, Dealer Activity, and Liquidity Risk*, The
Journal of Finance, Vol. 34 No. 3, June (1979), pp.
577-593

Goldman, M Barry and Avraham Beja, Market Prices Vs.
*Equilibrium Prices: Returns' Variance, Serial
Correlation, and the Role of the Specialist*, The
Journal of Finance, Vol. 34 No. 3, June, (1979), pp.
595-607

Granger, Clive, W.J., and Oskar Morgenstern,
Predictability of Stock Market Prices, Heath
Lexington Books, Lexington, MA, (1970), 303 pages

Grant, Rebecca A., *Building and Testing a Causal Model
of an Information Technology's Impact*, Proceedings
of the Tenth International Conference on Information
Systems, (1989) pp. 1173-184

Grossman, Sanford and Merton Miller, *The Determinants
of Market Liquidity*, CRSP Working Paper (1986)

Grossman, S.J., *Analysis of the Implications for Stock
and Futures Price Volatility of Program Trading and
Dynamic Hedging Strategies*, The Journal of
Business, July (1988) pp. 275-298

Grossman, S.J., *Program Trading and Market Volatility: A Report on Intraday Relationships*, Financial Analysts Journal, Vol. 44 No. 4, July (1988) pp. 18-28

Hakansson, Nils H., Avraham Beja, and Jivendra Kale, *On the Feasibility of Automatic Market Making by a Programmed Specialist*, The Journal of Finance, Vol. 11 No. 1, March (1985)

Hamilton, James L., *Electronic Market Linkages and the Distribution of Order Flow: the Case of the Off-Board Trading of NYSE Listed Stocks*, in Lucas and Schwartz (1989) pp. 263-285

Hamilton, James L., *Off-Board Trading of NYSE Listed Stocks: The Effect of Deregulation and the National Market System*, The Journal of Finance, Vol. 42 No. 5, Dec (1987) pp. 1331-1345Harris, Lawrence, "Estimation of True Price Variances and Bid-Ask Spreads from Discrete Observations", Working Paper, University of Southern California, (1985)

Harris, S.E. and J.L. Katz, *Profitability and Information Technology Capital Intensity in the Insurance Industry*, Proceedings of the Twenty First Hawaii International Conference on System Sciences, January (1988) pp. 124-130

Hasbrouck, Joel and Thomas S.Y.Ho, *Order Arrival, Quote Behavior, and the Return-Generating Process*, The Journal of Finance, September (1987), pp. 1035-1048

Hasbrouck, Joel and Robert A. Schwartz, *Liquidity and Execution Costs in Equity Markets*, The Journal of Portfolio Management, Spring (1988) pp. 10-16

Hasbrouck, Joel, *Measuring the Information Content of Stock Trades*, The Journal of Finance, March (1991), pp. 179-207

Heffernan, Shelagh A., *A Characteristics Definition of Financial Markets*, Journal of Banking and Finance, V. 14 (1990), pp. 583-609

Hilton, Ronald W., *The Determinants of Information Value: Synthesizing Some General Results*, Management Science, Vol. 27 No.1, Jan (1981) pp. 57-64

Hirschheim, Rudy and Heinz K. Klein, *Four Paradigms of Information Systems Development*, Communications of the ACM, Vol. 32 (1988) pp. 1199-1216

Ho, Thomas and Richard Macris, *Dealer Market Structure and Performance*, in Amihud, Ho, and Schwartz (1985) pp. 41-66

Ho, Thomas S.Y., Robert a Schwartz, and David K. Whitcomb, *The Trading Decision and Market Clearing under Transaction Price Uncertainty*, The Journal of Finance, March (1985), pp. 21-29

Hunter, Samuel E., *Arbitrage Trading*, in Amihud, Ho, and Schwartz (1985) pp. 145-150

Jang, Hasung and C. Venkatesh, *Consistency between Predicted and Actual Bid-Ask Quote Revisions*, The Journal of Finance, March (1991), pp. 433-445

Jensen, M.C., and W.H. Meckling, *Theory of the Firm: Managerial Behavior, Agency Costs, and Ownership Structure*, Journal of Financial Economics, Vol. 3 (1976) pp. 305-360

Jonscher, Charles., *Information Resources and Economic Productivity*, Information Economics and Policy, Vol. 1 (1983) pp. 13-35

Kandt, Kirk and Paul Yuenger, *A Financial Investment Assistant*, in Trippi and Turban (1990), pp. 62-77

Kaplan, B. and D. Duchon, *Combining Qualitative and Quantitative Methods in Information System Research*, MIS Quarterly, Vol. 12 No. 4, Dec (1988)

Kawaller, I.G., P.D. Koch, and D.W. Koch, *The Temporal Price Relationship between the S&P500 Futures and the S&P500 Index*, The Journal of Finance, December (1987), pp. 1309-1329

Keen, P.G.W., *MIS Research: Reference Disciplines and Cumulative Tradition*, Proceedings of the First International Conference on Information Systems, (1980) pp. 10-23

King, William R. and James I Rodriguez, *Evaluating Management Information Systems*, MIS Quarterly, Sep. (1978) pp. 43-51

Kruchten, D., *Expert Systems in Trading and Trading Exposure Management*, in Proceedings of the First Annual Conference on Expert Systems in Business and Finance, IEEE, (1987)

Lee, Charles M.C. and Mark J. Ready, *Inferring Trade Directions from Intraday Data*, The Journal of Finance, June (1991), pp. 733-746

Lucas, Henry, *Performance and Use of and Information System*, Management Science Vol. 21 (1975a) pp. 908-918

Lucas, Henry, *The Use of an Accounting Information System, Action, and Organizational Performance*, The Accounting Review, October (1975b), pp. 735-746

Lucas, Henry C. and Robert Schwartz, *The Challenge of Information Technology for the Securities Markets: Liquidity, Volatility, and Global Trading*, Dow Jones-Irwin, Homewood, IL, (1989)

Louis, Arthur M., *The Stock Market of the Future - Now*, Fortune, Oct. 29 (1984) pp. 105-318

Macklin, Gordon S., *The Financial Services Industry of Tomorrow*, The National Association of Securities Dealers, Inc., Washington, DC, November, (1982)

Malone, Thomas W., JoAnne Yates, and Robert Benjamin, *Electronic Markets and Electronic Hierarchies: Effects of Information Technology on Market Structures and Corporate Strategies*, Proceedings of the Seventh International Conference on Information Systems, (1986) pp. 109-112

Mandelbrot, Benoit, *The Variation of Certain Speculative Prices*, Journal of Business, Vol. 36, October, (1963), pp. 394-419

Mansfield, Edwin, *Technical Change and the Rate of Imitation*, Econometrica, Vol. 29 No. 4, Oct. (1961)

Markus, M.L., *Power, Politics, and MIS Implementation*, Communications of the ACM, Vol. 26, June (1983), pp. 430-444

Marshall, Roger W. and Steven C. Carlson, *Electronic Trading Systems: the User's Point of View*, in Amihud, Ho, and Schwartz (1985) pp.285-295

Matteson, Frederick E., *What October 19 Almost Showed Us*, Information Strategy the Executive's Journal, Vol. 5 No. 1, Fall (1988), pp. 4-8

McFarlan, F.W. and J.L. McKenney, *The Information Archipelago - Gaps and Bridges*, Harvard Business Review, Vol. 60 No. 5 (1982) pp. 109-119

Meeker, J.E., *The Work of the Stock Exchange*, The Ronald Press Company, New York, (1930)

Melone, Nancy Paule, *A Theoretical Assessment of the User-Satisfaction Construct in Information Systems Research*, Management Science, Vol. 36 No. 1, Jan (1990)

Miller, Edward M., *Explaining Intra-Day and Overnight Price Behavior*, The Journal of Portfolio Management, Summer (1989), pp. 10-16

Miller, Edward M., *Explaining Intra-Day and Overnight Price Behavior: Reply to Comment*, The Journal of Portfolio Management, Winter (1989), pp. 87-88

Miller, Jonathan, *Information Systems Effectiveness: The Fit Between Business Needs and System Capabilities*, Proceedings of the Tenth International Conference on Information Systems, (1989) pp. 273-288

Miller, Merton, *Financial Innovation: The Last Twenty Years and the Next*, Journal of Financial and Quantitative Analysis, Vol. 21 No. 4, Dec (1986) pp. 459-471

Mumford, E., *Research Methods in Information Systems*, Elsevier Science Publishers, North Holland (1985)

Munshi, Jamal, *MIS: Cases in Action,* McGraw Hill Book Company, NY, (1990)

Munshi, Jamal, *The Diffusion of Innovation in the Retail Industry*, Poceedings of the Western Decision Sciences Institute Annual Meeting, 1994, Maui, Hawaii, (1994)

Munshi, Jamal, *A Framework for MIS Effectiveness*,Proceedings of the Decision Sciences Institute, Houston, (1991)

NASD, *NASDAQ/London International Link: A Guide for Level 2/3 Subscribers*, The National Association of Securities Dealers, (1987)

Neal, Robert, *Potential Competition and Actual Competition in Equity Options*, The Journal of Finance, V. XLII n. 3, July (1987), pp. 511-531

Newman, Michael, *Quality of Markets: The London Experience* in Lucas and Schwartz (1989) pp. 224-231

Osborne, M.F.M, *The Dynamics of Stock Trading*,Econometrica, Vol. 33, January (1965)

Niederhoffer, Victor and M.F.M. Osborne, *Market Making and Reversal on the Stock Exchange*, Journal of the American Statistical Association, v. 61 n. 316 December (1966), pp. 897-916

Noland, R. and H. Seward, *Measuring User Satisfaction to Evaluate Information Systems*, in R.L. Roland, editor, "Managing the Data Resource Function, West Publishing Company, Los Angeles, (1974)

NYSE, *Fact Book*, New York Stock Exchange, Inc., (1990), 98 pages

Osborne, M.F.M., *The Dynamics of Stock Trading*, Econometrica, v. 33 No. 1 January (1965), pp. 88-113

Peake, Junius W., Morris Mendelson, and R. T. Williams, *Black Monday: Market Structure and Market Making*, in Lucas and Schwartz (1989) pp. 159-199

PIMS Program: *Management Productivity and Information Technology*, The Strategic Management Institute, Cambridge, MA, (1984)

Plot, Charles R. and Michael D. Johnson, *The Effect of Two Trading Institutions on Price Expectations and the Stability of Supply-Response Lag Markets*, The Journal of Economic Psychology, Vol. 10 (1989) pp. 189-216

Powell, Doug, *Toward the Automated Stock Exchange*, Computing Canada, Vol. 15 No. 21, Oct. 12, (1989) pp. 1-4

Racioppo, Stephen G., *Expert Systems in Global Financial Markets*, in Trippi and Turban (1990), pp. 39-46

Rappaport, Stephen P., *Management on Wall Street: Making Securities Firms Work*, Dow Jones-Irwin, Homewood, IL, (1988)

Riess, Robert N., *NASDAQ: Experience With Pioneering an Electronic Market*, in Lucas and Schwartz (1989) pp. 214-223

Roll, Richard, *A Simple Implicit Measure of the Effective Bid-Ask Spread in an Efficient Market*, The Journal of Finance, September (1984), pp. 1127-1139

Roll, Richard, *The International Crash of 1987*, Financial Analysts Journal, Vol. 44 No. 5, Sep. (1988) pp. 19-35

Romberg, John S., Edward J. Dudewicz, Pandu R. Tadikamalla, and Edward F. Mykytka, *A Probability Distribution and its Uses in Fitting Data*, Technometrics, Vol. 21, No. 2, May (1979), pp. 201-214

Saunders, Anthony, and Lawrence J. White, *Technology and the Regulation of Financial Markets*, Lexington Books, Lexington, MA, (1986), 193 pages.

SEC, *Report of the Special Study of Securities Markets of the SEC Part II*, 88th Congress, First Session, House Document Number 95, Part 2, US Govt Printing Office July 17, (1963)

Schreiber, Paul S. and Robert A. Schwartz, *Efficient Price Discovery in a Securities Market: The Objective of a Trading System*, in Amihud, Ho, and Schwartz (1985) pp.19-39

Schwartz, Robert A., *Comment on Market Automation* in Saunders and White (1986) pp. 57-59

Schwartz, Robert A., *Equity Markets: Structure, Trading, and Performance*, Harper and Row, New York, (1988)

Schwert, G. William, *Stock Market Volatility*, Financial
  Analysts Journal, May-June, (1990), pp. 23-34
Scribner, Richard O., *The Technological Revolution in
  Securities Trading*, in Saunders and White (1986) pp.
  19-29
Sethi, Vijay and William R. King, *Construct
  Measurement in Information Systems Research*,
  Decision Sciences, July/August (1991), pp. 455-472
Sharda, Ramesh, Steve H. Barr, and James C. McDonnel,
  Decision Support System Effectiveness, Management
  Science, Vol. 34 (1988) pp. 139-159
Simon, H., *A Behavioral Model of Rational Choice*,
  Quarterly Journal of Economics, Vol. 69 (1955) pp.
  99-118
Smidt, S., *Which Road to an Efficient Stock Market: Free
  Competition or a Regulated Monopoly?*, Financial
  Analysts Journal, v. 27, (1971) pp. 18-20
Smidt, Seymour, *Productivity, Technological Change,
  and Futures Trading*, in Saunders and White (1986),
  pp. 79-94
Sobel, Robert, *The Big Board: A History of the New
  York Stock Exchange*, The Free Press, New York,
  (1965)
Srinavasan, Ananth, *Alternative Measures of System
  Effectiveness*, MIS Quarterly, September (1985) pp.
  243-253
Stigler, George, *The Division of Labor is Limited to the
  Extent of the Market*, Journal of Political Economy,
  June (1951) pp. 185-193
Stigler, George, *The Economics of Information*, Journal
  of Political Economy, June (1961)
Stoll, Hans R., *Alternative Views of Market Making*, in
  Amihud, Ho, and Schwartz (1985) pp. 67-91
Stoll, Hans R., *The Stock Exchange Specialist System:
  An Economic Analysis*, Monograph Series in
  Finance and Economics, Monograph No. 1985-2,
  Graduate School of Business and Economics, New
  York University, (1985), 53 pages.

Stoll, Hans R. and Henry F. Minnerop, *Technological Change in the Back Office: Implications for Structure and Regulation of the Securities Industry*, in Saunders and White (1986) pp. 31-59

Stoll, Hans E. and Robert E. Whaley, *Program Trading and Expiration Day Effects*, Financial Analysts Journal, Vol. 32 No. 2, Mar (1987) pp. 16-28

Strassman, P.A., *Value-Added Productivity Measurement: Concepts and Results*, EDP Analyzer, v. 22 no. 2 June (1984) pp. 13-14

Tam, Kar Yan, *Computer Based Security Trading Systems*, Journal of Information Science Principles & Practice, Vol. 15 No. 6, (1989) pp. 345-354

Treacy, Michael E., *Toward a Behaviorally Grounded Theory of Information Value*, Proceedings of the Eighth International Conference on Information Systems, (1987) pp. 247-257

Treacy, Michael, and Soonchul Lee, *The Impact of Information Technology on Control: A Leadership Theory Perspective*, Proceedings of the Eighth International Conference on Information Systems, (1987) pp. 442-453

Trice, Andrew W. and Michael E. Treacy, *Utilization as a Dependent Variable in MIS Research*, Proceedings of the Seventh International Conference on Information Systems, (1986) pp. 10-23

Trippi, Robert R. and Efraim Turban, Investment Management: *Decision Support and Expert Systems*, Boyd and Fraser Publishing Company, Boston (1990)

Turner, J., *Organizational Performance, Size, and the Use of Data Processing Resources*, Working Paper #58, Center for Research on Information Systems, New York University, NY, (1985)

Van Horn, R.L., *Empirical Studies in MIS*, Database, Winter (1973)

Van Kirk, Robert A., *How SIAC Survived*, in Lucas and Schwartz (1989) pp. 240-246

Vickrey, William, *Counterspeculation, Auctions, and Competitive Sealed Tenders*, The Journal of Finance, V.16, (1961) pp. 8-37

Vitalari, N.P., *The Need for Longitudinal Designs in the Study of Information Systems*, in Mumford (1985) pp. 271-280

Von Neumann J. and O. Morgenstern, *Theory of Games and Economic Behavior*, Princeton University Press, Princeton, NJ, (1944)

Wagner, Wayne, *Complete Guide to Securities Transactions*, John Wiley and Sons, New York (1988)

Wall, John T., *The Competitive Environment of the Securities Market*, in Amihud, Ho, and Schwartz (1985) pp.131-144

Walras, Leon, *Elements of Pure Economics*, (1874), William Jaffe translation, R.D. Irwin, Homewood, IL, (1954)

Weill, Peter, and Margarethe H. Olson, *Managing Investment in Information Technology: Mini Case Examples and Implications*, MIS Quarterly, March, (1989) pp. 3-9

Whitcomb, David K., *An International Comparison of Stock Exchange Trading Securities*, in Amihud, Ho, and Schwartz (1985) pp. 237-255

Williams, Stephen L., *The Evolving National Market System*, in Amihud, Ho, and Schwartz (1985) pp. 257-268

Williamson, O.E., *Markets and Hierarchies*, The Free Press, New York, (1975)

Wood R.A., T. McInish, and J. Ord, *An Investigation of Transactions Data for NYSE Stocks*, The Journal of Finance, vol: 40, pp. 723-741 (1985)

Index

automation 1, 4, 6, 9, 14, 15, 26, 28, 30, 31, 32, 38, 46, 69, 70, 71, 72, 74, 87

case study 3, 4, 15, 19, 20, 31, 69, 72
circuit breaker 30, 71
CLOB 6, 30, 32
computer 1, 3, 4, 9, 16, 28, 30, 31, 71, 72, 74, 75, 77, 78, 88

EDB 36, 38, 44, 46, 47, 51, 53, 54, 57, 59, 60, 61, 63, 65, 68, 69, 70
efficient market 5, 70, 86
excess .i.volatility 37
excess volatility 27, 34, 35, 36, 37, 38, 46, 47, 48, 50, 51, 53, 54, 55, 58, 59, 61, 63, 66, 67, 68, 70

Information systems 1, 2, 15, 69, 71, 75, 79, 80, 81, 82, 83, 84, 85, 86, 87, 89
intervention 12, 20, 39, 43, 44, 53, 54, 76
intraday volatility 1, 14, 25, 34, 35, 38, 40, 47, 50, 54, 58
IT effectiveness 1, 2, 18

least square mean 43, 61, 63
limit order 6, 7, 8, 9, 12, 21, 22, 24, 30, 32, 34, 36, 38, 70, 72
Linear Model 35, 38, 42, 48, 49, 50, 52, 54, 55, 58
liquidity 4, 5, 6, 7, 8, 9, 11, 24, 27, 29, 30, 31, 33, 36, 39, 41, 46, 52, 64, 65, 70, 71, 74, 78, 79, 81, 82, 84

market order 8, 12, 22, 30
market quality 6, 9, 12, 14, 15, 28, 46, 71

measure 2, 5, 14, 16, 21, 24, 25, 34, 37, 52, 70, 79, 86
microstructure 1, 4, 6, 15, 20, 23, 25, 34, 38, 47, 69, 71, 72, 74, 75

NASDAQ 6, 28, 32, 77, 79, 85, 86
NYSE 1, 4, 6, 7, 8, 9, 11, 20, 21, 22, 23, 25, 27, 28, 31, 36, 43, 46, 49, 51, 69, 70, 72, 74, 75, 81, 82, 86, 90

price behavior 1, 12, 15, 22, 23, 24, 25, 35, 38, 69, 70, 74, 85
price volatility 8, 13, 21, 24, 25, 27, 36, 39, 46, 47, 48, 55, 69, 70, 71, 81

screen trading 6, 31, 71, 72
social paradigm 15
specialist 1, 4, 6, 7, 8, 9, 10, 11, 12, 13, 21, 22, 23, 24, 25, 26, 29, 30, 31, 32, 34, 36, 37, 38, 40, 41, 48, 50, 52, 53, 56, 59, 64, 70, 71, 74, 75, 81, 88

tick 11, 52, 64
trading mechanism 1, 4, 5, 6, 7, 10, 11, 12, 15, 20, 22, 23, 26, 27, 28, 69

volatility 1, 4, 5, 6, 8, 9, 11, 12, 13, 14, 15, 20, 23, 24, 26, 27, 28, 29, 30, 33, 34, 36, 37, 39, 41, 43, 45, 46, 52, 53, 64, 69